Citizenship & Person-Centered Work

with

Beth Mount • Diana Whitney

Michael Smull • Denise Bissonnette

Jack Pearpoint • Mike Green

Connie Ferrell • John O'Brien

Editors   Volume III

John O'Brien & Carol Blessing

INCLUSION

Library and Archives Canada Cataloguing in Publication

Conversations on citizenship & person-centred work / edited by John O'Brien & Carol Blessing.

Includes bibliographical references and index.

ISBN 978-1-895418-87-3

    1. People with disabilities--Services for. 2. People with disabilities--Social conditions. 3. People with disabilities--Employment. 4. Social integration. I. O'Brien, John, 1946- II. Blessing, Carol

HV1568.C65 2011   362.4   C2011-905075-7

Cover Photo: That luang gate in Vientiane, Laos. Jack Pearpoint

Cornell University
ILR School
Employment and Disability Institute

© 2011 Inclusion Press
All Rights Reserved

This materials in this book were developed, in part, with sponsorship from the New York State Office of Mental Health, Career Development Initiative, (contract number C008294) and in collaboration with the School of Industrial and Labor Relations Employment and Disability Institute at Cornell University.

Published by Inclusion Press in collaboration with Cornell University

Copyright © 2011 Inclusion Press

All rights reserved. No part of this publication may be produced, stored in a retrieval system or transmitted, in any form or by any means electronic, mechanical, photocopying, recording or otherwise, without the prior written permission from the publisher.

Printed in Canada by Couto Printing & Publishing
Printed on stock containing post consumer recycled content

INCLUSION PRESS
47 Indian Trail, Toronto
Ontario Canada M6R 1Z8
p. 416.658.5363 f. 416.658.5067
inclusionpress@inclusion.com

inclusion.com   BOOKS •WORKSHOPS • MEDIA • RESOURCES

Contents

Thanks	8
Carol Blessing	
Citizen-Centered Leadership	9
John O'Brien	
Some common threads	19
Beth Mount	23
What is citizenship?	23
What keeps people with disabilities from full citizenship?	23
What is community?	24
What inspires you?	24
What drew you into this work?	25
What makes a positive difference in the lives of people in services?	25
What is leadership?	26
What does it mean to be person-centered?	26
Why is courage important in person-centered work?	26
How did Personal Futures Planning begin?	27
What were your intentions in developing Personal Futures Planning?	27
How do participants in Personal Futures Planning connect to their community?	29
What role does art play in your work?	29
Diana Whitney	33
What is Appreciative Inquiry?	33
Where did Appreciative Inquiry come from?	36
Tell us about Appreciative Inquiry as a methodology.	37
What are the core principles of Appreciative Inquiry?	39
What has Appreciative Inquiry taught you about leadership?	41
What strategies implement Appreciative Leadership?	43
Michael Smull	45
What inspires you?	45
What drew you into your work?	45

What are the origins of Essential Lifestyle Planning? 45
Is person-centered planning just for people with
    developmental disabilities? 47
Are there circumstances in which you shouldn't do a plan? 47
How did the person-centered thinking skills develop? 47
How do person-centered thinking skills contribute
    to change in organizations and systems? 49
Please describe the person-centered thinking skills. 51
How do you respond to people who say that
    person-centered skills are too costly to implement? 53
How can we track development in the service system? 54

Denise Bissonnette 57
    What is citizenship? 59
    What has kept people with disabilities from citizenship? 60
    What is leadership? 60
    What inspires you? 61
    How can people make a positive difference? 61
    What is community? 62
    How does somebody actually build community? 62
    What does work mean to you? 62
    What impact has the ADA had? 63
    What differences do you see between traditional
        job placement and true job development? 63
    Why would an employer create or carve a position? 65
    What do we need to keep in mind in order to keep true
        partnerships with employers? 66
    What support is important for the person who wants
        to work? 67
    How do you support people to develop those skills? 67
    Can you give us a feel for the *Cultivating True Livelihood*
        curriculum? 69
    What does it take to sustain us in this work? 71

Jack Pearpoint   75
    What have been some of the important influences on your work?   75
    What does it mean to be person-centered?   76
    What does person-centered planning have to do with people's disabilities?   76
    Tell us about your early involvement with person-centered approaches.   76
    What was your first approach to person-centered planning?   77
    How does exclusion affect person-centered planning?   78
    How do you know person-centered planning is working?   79
    Are there times when person-centered planning does not work?   79
    What are the risks of person-centered planning?   79
    What is MAPS?   80
    What is PATH and how is it different from MAPS?   81
    What's important in preparing for MAPS or PATH?   83
    How do you choose between MAPS and PATH?   83
    How do you address the concern that person-centered planning takes too long and costs too much?   84
    How do we build community?   84

Mike Green   87
    Where did Asset Based Community Development (ABCD) come from?   87
    Your work is in community organizing, what interests you about person-centered work?   88
    What does citizenship mean to you?   88
    Isn't citizenship for people with disabilities a right and not an option?   89
    How does ABCD compliment person-centered practices?   89
    How does ABCD increase people's potential to experience citizenship?   91
    What assets should we be looking for in a community?   92
    What contribution does asset mapping make?   92
    What is a capacity inventory?   94
    Tell us about social networks.   95

Say more about associational life. 95
What does it take to make connections between people with
 disabilities and community associations? 96
How can organizations become a real resource to their
 communities? 96

Connie Ferrell 99
How does our society view people with disabilities? 99
What does it mean to belong to a community? 100
How do staff make a positive difference? 100
How do you see leadership? 100
What is supported employment? 101
What are the principles of effective supported employment? 102
How is a person-centered approach to people with disabilities
 different from other approaches? 103
How do you see the difference between person-centered planning
 and person-centeredness? 105
What do we have to give up in order to move to
 person-centered work? 106
What is the Framework for Planning? 107

John O'Brien 109
What is disability? 109
Why citizenship important for people with disabilities? 110
What keeps people with disabilities from being full citizens
 with access to valued community roles? 111
How does all this matter to person-centered work? 113
What is leadership? 114
What place does courage have in social innovation? 115
How has innovation in service provision affected
 person-centered work? 117
How can we minimize stereotypes and biases against people
 with disabilities? 118
What is discrimination? 119
How does poverty affect person-centered work? 120
What is the principle of normalization? 120
How did the principle of normalization influence the development of
 person-centered planning? 122

How do you judge the effectiveness of person-centered work?	123
What is the purpose of person-centered work?	126
What's the difference between person-centered work and typical service practice?	127
Are there people for whom person-centered planning doesn't work?	129
What conditions increase the effectiveness of person-centered work?	130

Index   135

Learning More   137

Implementing Person-Centered Planning: Voices of Experience	137
A Little Book About Person-Centered Planning	141

Images by Beth Mount

Make Your Mark	31
Learn the Neighborhood	32
Celebrate Relationships	56
Raise Expectations	74
Celebrate Community	86
Listen With Heart	98
Build Alliances	134

Thanks

We are deeply grateful to the participants in these interviews who agreed to share their thoughts in book form and approved the edited versions that appear here, and to the people who directed, arranged logistics, shot the video, recorded the sound, edited the video, and transcribed the interview tapes.

The chapters contained in this book have been edited from a series of interviews that were conducted between April – July, 2010 in conjunction with the Cornell University, School of Industrial and Labor Relations Employment and Disability Institute "Citizen-Centered Leadership Development" Community of Practice series (www.citizencentereedleadership.org). These interviews were sponsored, in part, by the New York State Office of Mental Health Career Development Initiative (COO8294). Special thanks to John Allegretti-Freeman who recognized the need for this work to come together for the good of us all.

Permissions

Thanks to Mayer Shevin for permission to reprint *The language of us and them* © 1987 on page 10, to Denise Bissonnette for permission to reprint *Blue Skies* on page 57 and *Rekindle the Flame* on page 71 and to Beth Mount for permission to reprint the fabric art on page 18, page 32, page 56, page 74, page 86, page 98, and page 134 (www.capacityworks for these and other images).

Photography Credits

Beth Mount, Denise Bissonnette, Connie Ferrell, and John O'Brien by Peter Bobrow, Bear Mountain Media

Carol Blessing by J. Blessing Photography

Jack Pearpoint and, Mike Green by Jeff Dobbin, Parashoot Productions, Inc

Diana Whitney by John Elkins

Carol Blessing
Citizen-Centered Leadership

The idea for what is becoming the Citizen-Centered Leadership Community of Practice has been percolating for a long time. Perhaps the first of the seeds was sown for me in 1987 with Mayer Shevin's poem "The Language of Us/Them", a timeless piece that boldly and irrefutably points to the artificial yet nevertheless impenetrable line that has been drawn between people who have labels of disability and those who do not. It was one of my first influences entering the field of human services. For me, two soulful questions lay underneath that poem: *What is the part I am playing in this? What is the collateral damage of our good intentions?*

Despite being armed with the critically important foundations of Wolf Wolfensberger's Theory of Normalization (and later the theory of Social Role Valorization), John O'Brien's Five Valued Experiences (an expression of citizenship through social equality), person-centered planning and community-building, and after years of working within the disability system, I have to say that most people in the services I know are honestly not much closer to living as full participants in our communities. There is a distinct "otherness" that surrounds people. *How can the experience of full community inclusion be so shaky when we are standing on such solid ground?*

Discomfort about this issue has been piling up for decades and it shows up across the face of many different situations. It is in the face of complacency when well-meaning service providers presume that all that is necessary to promote the full inclusion of people with disabilities has been done; that we are all "trained up." It is in the face of authority that mandates policies and procedures that are couched in the rhetoric of "best practices" and current politically correct language but do little to support the development of human potential and fail to recognize that a system is organic, comprised of living, breathing, brilliantly talented people inside and out. It is in the face of a society that is paralyzed by the belief that the human service delivery system must be the gatekeeper to community, must be the expert who can best translate the language of disability to the rest of the populace. It is in the faces of people with disabilities and their families who have come to accept this professional control as truth.

The Language of Us/Them
Mayer Shevin

We like things
 They fixate on objects
We try to make friends
 They display attention seeking behavior
We take breaks
 They display off task behavior
We stand up for ourselves
 They are non-compliant
We have hobbies
 They self-stim
We choose our friends wisely
 They display poor peer socialization
We persevere
 They perseverate
We like people
 They have dependencies on people
We go for a walk
 They run away
We insist
 They tantrum
We change our minds
 They are disoriented and have short attention spans
We have talents
 They have splinter skills
We are human
 They are . . . ?

All of this and more have forced other questions to emerge: *What is reinforcing and perpetuating this phenomenon? How do you dismantle a belief system that has been institutionalized? How do you encourage transformation that heals rather than harms, that strengthens rather than weakens our relationship to humanity? And for me, the most important question of all: what universal principal(s), if embraced, would serve to unite us all and render the line between Us/Them unacceptable?*

"Comes the dawn." My dad used that expression whenever I finally caught on to something rather obvious, something right in front of me. In this case, "the dawn" emerged as I identified the two social constructs of community that are most common in contemporary Western society: the disability model and the consumer model. In the disability model, oftentimes called the medical model, people are seen primarily through the lens of neediness and services are essential to address something that is wrong or sick or broken in them. This approach has embedded within it a system of paid experts and authorities who implement strategies and interventions designed to, at most, ameliorate or, at least, improve a particular condition. Those who experience disability as a temporary condition are able to move through the medical model system and resume life as expressed through the consumer model. Those who experience disability as a permanent condition generally rely quite heavily on the disability system and that system becomes central in their lives. In the disability model, the system dictates how its limited resources can be used to address what it defines as the person's needs. For individuals who look to the system for support, this creates, albeit unintentionally, powerlessness and dependency.

The consumer model is quite the opposite. Consumerism is a social and economic order that is centered on a person's wants and their ability to purchase goods and services. There is an underlying premise that the free choice of consumers should dictate the economic structure of a society. At its simplest level power to drive the system is in the hands of the people who have the resources to pick and choose the goods and services that they feel best meet their desires, interests and needs.

Here's the rub for people who have significant disabilities: most people who fall within this category are often called "consumers" in the disability model, but they lack the power to drive the system. The system determines and controls the goods and services that will be provided. So to be a consumer in this model implies something quite different than it does in a buyer's market –it implies using up resources. And because people with disabilities are often living at or near poverty levels, even those who have managed to live primarily in the community-based consumer model lack adequate resources to purchase the life that they imagine. Instead they experience consumerism as a spectator sport.

There is something fundamentally missing in both of these models, a profound absence of something much, much bigger than enticing people to want to buy more goods and services, or to buy-in to the notion that people need to be fixed somehow. In either model, though especially evident in the disability model, there seems to be an exemption from the social contract of citizenship. And authentic embodiment of citizenship may be at least one universal principle that serves to unite all people, that knows in its bones that it's okay for people to be just who they are. So "citizen-centered leadership" posits that in the struggle to support people with disabilities in reaching toward their highest potential as true citizens of the nation in the best possible way, we must look to our standards of citizenship to guide our standards of care and choices for best practices.

The United States was built on the bedrock of governance of the people, by the people, for the people and preserves the right to life, liberty and the pursuit of happiness. The democratic ideal that all people are created equal, that all people are entitled to equal opportunity to reach their highest purpose and that all people have the birth right and the responsibility to work toward the greater good is the social contract of citizenship and the standard by which decisions should be made and success measured. And yet social inequality rings louder than any Liberty Bell could.

The disability model, in many of its sectors, has adopted person-centered planning as a specific approach to developing service plans with people. The methods and tools associated with person-centered planning can be quite valuable in informing the system about where to align its resources to be of optimal service to supporting a person towards reaching a personally defined quality of life. However, the degree to which the information that surfaces through the planning process actually leads to higher level quality of life outcomes depends dramatically on who is defining the standard of success. If the authority governing a particular system is measuring success against the latest, greatest best practice coming from the medical field, then people's needs and interests will be forced to fit within that structure, with honest attempts to accommodate the person-centered direction when possible. If measured by the standard of citizenship, person-centered planning holds great potential for exploring how the personal aspirations of life, liberty and the pursuit of happiness held by people who use disability services might find expression in the community at large.

All over the world more and more people are recognizing that necessary deep change in the systems we count on occurs only in relationship to other human beings in the context of community. Engaging in purposeful conversations with other people who care deeply about an issue yields powerful, productive alternatives to maintaining systems that no longer work. The question of citizenship as it relates to people who have customarily been left at the margins of society and what it would take to move against the tide of Us/Them was the subject of the series of conversations in the spring and summer of 2010. In edited form, these conversations form this book.

To inform the online course, Citizen-Centered Leadership Development (www.citizencenteredleadership.org)I invited eight leaders who have influenced me and the fields of organization change and supports to the citizenship of people with disabilities. I selected them first because I see each of them as a pioneer, an inventor, an explorer, and sometimes a warrior, bushwhacking uncharted territory in the name of creating healthy, holistic communities that welcome, honor and celebrate the gifts of all of their members. Second, these individuals hold an important history; their experience spans four decades of learning from action. What they have learned can serve to ground us even as it launches us into the next generation of learning. Third, each is a remarkable teacher and mentor. The content of their work is uniquely and distinctly their own, single brilliant stars, yet the spirit-thread messages of belonging, capacity-building, strength, potential, and interdependent relationships weave their work together in a way that reaches far beyond the limit of any one individual. It is when we can align these stars in our own configurations that we can build life-giving relationships. This alignment to provoke systemic and social change with people on the fringe is hard work. It can be lonely work. It takes courage to step up to the plate, to work toward a higher purpose, our own and in service to others.

Too often middle management and direct line staff are expected to hold up more than their share of learning and practicing the latest innovation or technology. Unfortunately, they are often left adrift –frustrated and disappointed because they are expected to do things that the current structure of the system can't support. Organizations that are seriously invested in making the shift from being system-centered to becoming citizen-centered must be willing to exert the effort that it will take to redesign the parts of the system that are holding people back, and to face head-on the challenge of crossing the divide between service life and community life.

An irrepressible advocate for the civil rights of all people, and particularly people with disabilities, **Beth Mount** (www.capacityworks.com), has been assisting systems, organizations, individuals, and families to create innovative options that promote positive images of people throughout her career. Beth's person-centered planning methodology, Personal Future's Planning, was the first of its kind to integrate the ideals of citizenship, translated as John O'Brien's Five Valued Accomplishments and Outcomes, into the heart of the planning process. Like John, Beth has a deep connection to the history of the disability rights movement and she has contributed her passion about this and about the urgent need to empower people with disabilities and those who support them toward imagining and moving to a positive future rich with contribution and belonging. Beth shares with us her expertise, her passion and provides practical tools for helping us to support people with disabilities toward "lives of distinction." Beth has devoted her entire career to transforming systems of care on behalf of and with individuals who rely on those services. She combines her remarkable talent as an artist into soulful work that throws open the windows and doors of creative potential to gives voice to people with disabilities, their families, direct support workers, management teams and whole organizations. Beth teaches how to weave the gifts of every human being into the fabric of community life.

The strength-based, capacity-driven, and evidence-based approach of Appreciative Inquiry and of Appreciative Leadership runs parallel to the philosophy of person-centered planning and community-building. **Diana Whitney** is the president of Corporation for Positive Change (www.positivechange.org) and a master in the art of revolutionary and transformational positive organizational change. She brings to our table the invitation and the opportunity to co-create life-giving organizations that ignite passion and excellence within and beyond their formal structure.

Michael Smull (www.elpnet.net) spent years working to support people whose significant disabilities were compounded by what he calls "severe reputations" move from institutional to community settings. The poverty of experience and social isolation inflicted on these people by the institution made existing approaches to person-centered planning a poor fit with the transition these people were making, so along with Susan Burke Harrison he created Essential Lifestyle Planning to specify the kinds of settings and supports people need for a good life in community services. Along with the other members of the international Learning Community for Person-Centered Thinking, Michael has refined and developed this approach into a set of person-centered thinking tools and a comprehensive approach to organizational development and system change.

The signature work of **Denise Bissonnette** (www.diversityworld.com) offers an innovative approach to assisting people in making the leap from grabbing at any job opportunity out there – almost surely destined to fail or breed discontent- to sculpting a livelihood that gathers together spirit and talent with keen awareness and appreciation of what a community deeply wants. Denise describes how to develop alternatives to traditional job development through creation of employment proposals that push people beyond barriers to possibility. She offers a variety of tools and resources collected in Cultivating True Livelihood. Denise, like Beth, brings her art into everything she does, using her words to weave images that gather us into the human experiences that can limit or liberate human potential.

A world leader in the arena of inclusion, **Jack Pearpoint** (www.inclusion.com) acts from the heart of community inclusion: a deep belief that everything and everyone is interconnected, each of us is important and everyone has a gift that is necessary for all of us to thrive. He serves as a pivotal and nimble conduit between human beings of all ages and from all walks of life. Internationally known as a facilitator, graphic artist and publisher, Jack describes the origins and descriptions of the MAPs and PATH planning process and the lessons of a lifetime of supporting development among people at the edges.

The disability service delivery system exists as an entity that is distinct from typical community. It is on the proverbial outskirts of town. It's "over there" where "those people" go. Healthy, intentional communities recognize that everyone has a place and everything has a purpose and a responsibility to serve the greater good. It is time that human service systems start contributing to and receiving from the whole of community and communities start seeing that the value of service systems is not to keep some people out, but to add to the richness of it. **Mike Green** (http://mike-green.org/) contributes his knowledge and expertise in Asset Based Community Development (ABCD) as the basis for organizing citizen-action to building more inclusive communities. Mike's clarity about what makes communities teem with abundance or wither from neglect is vital to our work in supporting people toward community life. Mike provides the tools and resources we need to see our neighborhoods as the "glass half full" and to discover the essence of what matters in the heart of any and every community. The underlying premise of ABCD is that all of the ingredients for building healthy, sustainable communities are already there. Exploring and understanding what the community has to offer and what it cares most about mobilizes people to take action that includes the talents and gifts of anyone and that benefit everyone. We need to shift our thinking from the idea that the community is something to work at so that people with disabilities become community members.

Employment is an expectation of citizenship. For people with significant impairments to going to work, an approach called supported employment has proven to be one of the best ways in assisting people who want to work find work that matches their interests and needs with opportunities in the competitive job market. **Connie Ferrell**, Integrated Services, was one of the pioneers of supported employment when it emerged in the form of demonstration projects in the late 1970's and early 1980's. Connie has devoted her career to learning and then teaching supported employment strategies and interventions that today are nationally recognized as best practice. In 2004, Connie co-developed a person-centered planning model that originally was designed to focus exclusively on finding direction for employment with people who were having a difficult time finding or keeping a job, but the Framework for Planning quickly and easily applied to areas outside employment as well, including organizational strategic thinking and planning.

A recognized name in the realm of person-centered planning, **John O'Brien** (www.inclusion.com/jobrien.html) has been involved in the development of several widely used person-centered planning processes. His essay "What's Worth Working For? Leadership for Better Quality Human Services," (1989)[*] has been important to me because it articulates central principles and clear outcomes that provide a foundation for person-centered work that embody democratic ideals. Increasing the valued experiences of sharing the ordinary places of community life, experiencing the respect that comes with playing valued social roles, developing competence and contributing, making choices, and belonging in a growing web of relationships and memberships guide both planning with people and developing organizational capacities.

---

[*] Download this essay at http://thechp.syr.edu/whatsw.pdf

Have Courage
See with the Eyes of the Heart

Beth Mount

John O'Brien
Some common threads

If we had not already used the title, this collection of interviews would have been called *Voices of Experience*.* Those who responded to Carol Blessing's invitation to reflect on their practice of supporting personal and organizational change have contributed to, and learned from, deep changes in their overlapping fields of organization development, community organizing, support for employment, and planning and working with people with disabilities in person-centered ways. Their work for social change has continued through decades, yet no one feels like their work is done.

Each voice in the chapters that follow is distinctive, but some common threads appear over and again. Here are eight.

The way we direct attention is fateful. Our work with people and communities and organizations makes a positive difference when it is grounded in attending with care to what people want more of, to what people care about, to what gives meaning and serves higher purpose, to gifts and capacities and interests, to what works as people take action. This kind of attention distinguishes the work represented in these interviews from a more common approach which encourages a focus on what people want to avoid, to diagnosing deep problems and enumerating deficiencies, to scheming about how to market and control and incentivize so people will do as they are told.

People with disabilities have important contributions to make to our common life. They have a right to discover their distinctive ways to exercise the responsibilities of active citizenship. It demeans people with disabilities and deprives our communities to cast them in passive roles as clients to be supervised and serviced or consumers to be satisfied. The proper role of human service, and the proper use of public money, is to support people to discover, develop, and deliver their contributions to the fami-

---

* On page 137, you can review the tables of contents from the two previous volumes in this series: *Implementing Person-Centered Planning: Voices of Experience* and *A Little Book about Person-Centered Planning*.

lies, workplaces, schools, neighborhoods, networks and associations that define our communities.

Too many people with disabilities are neither seen nor treated as contributing citizens. Instead, an elaborate command and control system based on a relentless focus on deficiencies in people with disabilities, their families, and their communities leaves those who count on its services to work out their lives in separate, professionally designed and organized worlds. The point of person-centered work and supported employment is to break open these constricting worlds. Laws like the Americans with Disabilities Act express the hopes of people with disabilities but leave a great deal of work to be done. This involves deconstructing both the most socially common narratives of disability as disease in search of cure and the physical and organizational designs that contain, control, and blunt the talents of people with disabilities and those who assist them. This deconstruction will be best guided by an appreciative focus that guides a creative search for meaning.

When citizenship is compromised, the trouble is not with people with disabilities or with community members. As younger people, those who speak here entered a field in turmoil over the place of people with disabilities in society. We have been personally and practically involved in rendering institutions unnecessary by creating local settings and good supports, in opening typical classrooms in neighborhood schools to new learners, in assisting those defined as unemployable into good jobs. There was a climate of controversy, conflict, and uncertainty about how to make things happen. Ways of assisting people were being invented as we went along. The situation was fluid and central controls were weaker and commanded less respect (or fear) than they currently do. In this situation we became more and more deeply impressed with the resilience and creativity of people with disabilities themselves. Many, many of the people we assisted accepted and improved our imperfect and sometimes clumsy efforts and greatly improved their lives. Despite high profile resistance and rejection, we also benefited from the willingness and ability of typical classmates, neighbors, and co-workers to join in the work of inclusion when it was about making a particular person welcome and successful. This is not theory, it is what we have lived.

The changes we want have taken far longer than we imagined they would. While large numbers of people with disabilities have the assistance they need to benefit from inclusive education, live in their own homes, and bring home pay from good jobs, larger numbers do not. What's more, the systems that dispense public money have grown rigid with detail complexity and too many of the service organizations that people count on remain stuck in patterns that reinforce separation and control. The challenge is to generate social innovation in a very constrained environment that seems to have lost a way to activate its higher purpose at the same time that its managers can't seem to avoid attaching the tags "person-centered" and "self-determined" to every activity. This climate breeds cynicism and caution where trust and courage are most needed.

Making the change we need takes leadership of a kind that engages everyone in the risky business of adapting to new possibilities. Waiting for a single hero to deliver change is no more useful than expecting an authority figure to guarantee that there will be no risks or failures.

We have less confidence in person-centered planning than readers might think we would. The problem is not with any of the approaches, which continue to set positive directions and generate good ideas for making progress when they are applied with mindfulness and care by people with good training. We lose confidence (and some of us become a bit testy) when person-centered plans are treated as a sort of mindless word magic, disconnected from a context in which people can act resourcefully on what the planning discloses as meaningful. Unless people have allies committed to supporting the next good steps along their life journey, not much can happen. If an organizational climate of avoidance of possibility and compliance with rules controls people and their allies, not much can happen even if an organization swallows person-centered planning whole. We see person-centered planning as a means to guide the personal creativity and organizational innovation necessary for people with disabilities to act in valued social roles as contributing citizens. Without commitment to build social contexts that can support this higher purpose, person-centered planning is a distraction.

The knowledge and energy we need is relational. The contribution that the practices associated with person-centered work and employment support can make to people with disabilities and their communities depends on what those of us who choose to offer assistance bring to the relationship. The primary task is supporting the person to convene people who have been or are open to being recruited into active support of a good future that includes the person's contributions. The more deeply this whole group can listen, the more strongly they believe in the person, the more vividly they can imagine possibilities, the more widely they are connected, the more creatively they can see ways to move forward, the more courageously they can enter into agreements that engage their integrity, the more likely cycles of planning and acting will generate good changes. Professional skill matters in working out the accommodations and forms of assistance that will be of most use in dealing with whatever difficulties people's disabilities may pose as they go about creating a positive future, but unless people have allies who are aligned with that future, professional skill is likely to be sterile. Assisting meaningful employment and working in a person-centered way are applied arts, developed in communities of practice and nourished by what can only be captured in poetry and imagery.

Beth Mount

What is citizenship?

Citizenship is related to three ideals of democracy that are at the core of person-centered work. First, all people are created equal, which means that everyone is equally entitled to reach for their higher purpose. Second, in order to reach for higher purpose there must be equal opportunities to do so. Third, our work as citizens is not simply to receive but to give back; not just to reach for our own higher purpose, but to do so in a way that contributes to the greater good. Pursuing these ideals strengthens society and enriches culture for us all.

What keeps people with disabilities from full citizenship?

There is a pattern in American culture that devalues and keeps out those who are seen as most vulnerable, most dependent, and most imperfect. That cultural pattern shuts a lot of people out of participation. In person-centered work we're trying to create opportunities for people to be respected and included in ways that change that pattern.

Otto Scharmer uses the term attentional violence, which is our capacity not to see people in terms of who they can become but only see to them in terms of our assumptions about the limitations imposed by the past. Breaking out of attentional violence requires that we see people in a completely different light, as capable of joining in meeting the demands of a positive future. When we see one another in light of what we can become, we can stop shutting doors, stop excluding and segregating people and start discovering opportunities to reach for our higher purposes.

What is community?

Community is a place on the ground around where you live and where you work, and it's where your people are. In community, people come together in all manner of associations and have the opportunity and the responsibility to be involved in civic life. So our first obligation and commitment to community is to a place and a set of relationships and associations. Community is a place of belonging where we can show up and make a difference in valued ways as citizens.

We can't have real community without diversity. Real community is a whole that works to include all people, their gifts and contributions as well as their conflicts and misunderstandings. Our communities are really missing something when people with disabilities are not there. It's central to my work to understand that every person brings an important contribution that we don't even know is missing until it begins to evolve.

So giftedness is not just something in the person, it evolves in relationship. Seeking to bring in the gifts of excluded people brings forth the qualities in community that are essential for everyone's capacities to emerge and grow. When the ability to welcome and encourage gifts grows, our communities become more deeply whole and richer for everyone.

Community is built on common interests, common passions and connections. So our first responsibility is to find and understand people's interests and gifts then to discover what's in the community that people can connect with.

What inspires you?

My inspiration comes completely from the people with disabilities and their families that I've had a chance to know and care for and about. Because there's nothing that's more inspiring than when I see people who are up against day-to-day struggles act on their passion to contribute, to be somebody, to work, and to do whatever it takes to change the situations they're in.

What I've learned from people with disabilities is that every person has a purpose in life and reaching for that purpose is the source of meaning. To be here on the earth in our communities, in relationship to each other is what life is about. And to see the reach that people with disabilities are willing to make in spite of the fact that other people have written off the possibility of their gift and don't see it. To see people stay focused on that reach when they have even a little bit of support, that is the greatest lesson and the greatest gift that I've received.

Also, I can't imagine doing this work without the greats of the world; Nelson Mandela, Martin Luther King. They inspire me because I see our work with people with disabilities as a civil rights effort.

What drew you into this work?

I grew up in the South during the civil rights movement in the time of desegregation. Those childhood roots form a sense that it's possible to change the social status of a group of people and that I can be a part of that change.

As a college student, I was a Vista volunteer in a program that gave me a chance to work with people with disabilities in a rural community in southern Georgia. Because this was before implementation of The Education of All Handicapped Children Act (Public Law 94-142), I was able to be a part of the movement of children and young people who were isolated and segregated because of disability into the community's public schools. That was a turning point. I thought, *What could be more important than making a good place in our communities for all people?*

What makes a positive difference in the lives of people in services?

There are so many ways to make a positive difference. The key is believing that every person has gifts and accepting our responsibility to encourage people to uncover those gifts and to find opportunities around every corner to support those gifts unfolding in action.

This means recognizing that people's families have resources to bring, that the communities that people live in are filled with places and people that will and can include them if we help as needed. And those of us who work in services have passions, inspiration, energy and determination to bring into people's lives. Our task is to put all these capacities together to create new opportunities.

What is leadership?

Leadership is having the passion and courage to do whatever it takes to make a difference for the people around you in your community. It's about commitment, action and partnership more than position, authority, role or control. It's about making things happen because you care about them.

What does it mean to be person-centered?

To be person-centered is to put the person in the middle of our thinking and get to know the person in fresh and vital ways that set the pattern for everything else we do in partnership with that person. It starts with getting to know a person and their family and the important people in their lives and growing an understanding that clarifies a positive vision for that person. Then we follow through in action, taking direction from the information, knowledge, and wisdom that comes from attending to the person's hopes and gifts.

The most interesting indicators of the effectiveness of working in a person-centered way are the stories of deep change in people's lives. I've tracked some people's stories for many years. When we do the whole of it well the stories are inspiring, they're evocative and they move all who get to hear them forward. When we're not doing the work well, we don't actually have powerful stories to tell.

Being person-centered isn't writing plans on paper. It's complex interaction of investments and commitments that leads to real change in people's lives. When we take person-centered work seriously, we take on the entire organizational and cultural structure that limits people's opportunities. If we're not willing to answer the call to a journey of deep change, then person-centered work will turn into something superficial and fragmented. Maybe it will sprinkle a little bit of extra this and that into people's lives, but it won't make the difference that we know is possible.

Why is courage important in person-centered work?

Those of us with a passion for person-centered work have to be partners with people with disabilities, who are still up against discrimination and prejudice that leads to rejection and segregation. It takes courage on the part of everyone who wants change, people with disabilities and workers alike, to believe in possibilities that others can't imagine and to take on the misunderstanding and rejection that people with disabilities face on a daily basis in a way that creates respect and belonging.

Working for social change in a person-centered way is not clinical or programmatic. It's everyday civil rights work and courage is at the core of it. We have to be bold to leave our comfort zones and make partnerships that break out of segregation and cross over into citizenship.

How did Personal Futures Planning begin?
Personal Futures Planning* began in the early 1980's in response to a group of young people with developmental disabilities who were leaving high school. They were the first generation of young people who had access to public education, but they faced the same old thinking about their futures that led to segregation and isolation. Personal Futures Planning was developed as a way to generate completely different possibilities for these young adults. It was a conversation with a person and their family and a way to learn about their community in order to generate an imaginative idea about their belonging in community, primarily through employment. The key element was a vision that included employment for every single person. This makes active discovery of neighborhood and community opportunities for work, membership, and belonging central to the process; it can't just be done in a conference room, it has to be done with the individual in their community.

What were your intentions in developing Personal Futures Planning?
Personal Futures Planning was designed as a process to change our assumptions about people and their futures in five important ways.

First, we wanted to shift the way we see people from a deficiency view to a capacity view. So the discovery process was designed to highlight and amplify the interest, preferences and hopes that people have for their life in the community.

---

* Beth Mount. P*erson-centered planning: Finding directions for change using personal futures planning.* www.capacityworks.com

Second, we wanted to join with people and their families to create an imaginative vision of contribution in the community, not just placement in a service. We wanted to really reach for possibility.

Third, we wanted to encourage the people who spent the most time with people to come together as a circle of support that would hold responsibility for the plans and action that would bring the person into community life. That contrasted with the common pattern of professionals who spent very little time with a person sitting in a room making plans and decisions without the person's real involvement. If the person or family couldn't be there, we would cancel the meeting because it doesn't make sense to do a plan without them.

Fourth, we wanted to move away from the assumption that communities are always rejecting and discriminatory and explore ways to understand and strengthen communities by intentionally, thoughtfully, building involvement and belonging. That makes learning about the local community as important, as interesting and as illuminating as getting to know the person and their family.

Fifth, we wanted people's personal plans to shape a process of innovation in services, as organizations adapted to supporting people to work and live as citizens of their communities, not clients kept within the walls of services.

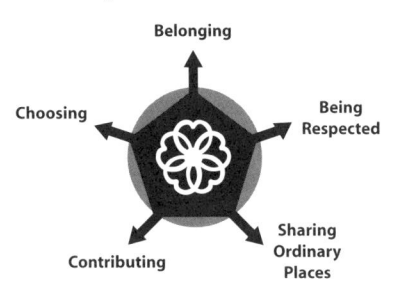

From the beginning, Personal Futures Planning has been guided by this star,[*] which represents what we are reaching for and gives us five windows into a good life in community that let us describe how things are now and consider how we want things to be. We also use the five points of the star to evaluate how we are doing. Are our actions resulting in the person being seen and treated respectfully and playing an active

---

[*] To learn more, see John O'Brien and Beth Mount (2005). *Make a Difference: A Guide to Person-Centered Direct Support*. Toronto: Inclusion Press. www.inclusion.com

part in ordinary community places? Is the person developing and contributing their gifts? Is the person making real choices? Does the person experience belonging?

How do participants in Personal Futures Planning connect to their community?

In Personal Futures Planning, community mapping isn't a theoretical exercise. Its actually getting out and covering the ground to become aware of what is right outside the door, down the street, and a bus ride away. It's important to do this on foot or on our wheels because there is a community that is invisible to drivers. There are many associations that won't show up in a directory, so we have to talk to local people to discover them. If a person cares about horses, we need to find the horse people and places. If a person cares about music, we need to find the music people and places. People may take along cameras and make a portrait of every community setting for a mile around that offers any potential for participation and contribution.

Then we do a community brainstorming exercise to look for where to start: given the person's gifts and interests, where's the first door to open. A support circle will often brainstorm fifteen or twenty possibilities. Then networking becomes important because the best places to start are places someone already has a connection to. Someone's brother's ex-wife is the cashier in that place or another person's mother knows someone who could smooth the person's way in. Networking isn't a hypothetical exercise, a chart to fill out. It's very specific to making living connections to places and associations and opportunities that will give a person a chance to participate and contribute.

What role does art play in your work?

For me art is an essential element of person-centered work. I think of the world in which we're connected and in which we walk with people as a multi-literate world. For the last twenty years most of my work has been in New York City where we speak a hundred and forty languages. People, their families, and support workers relate to their world at many different levels of literacy and through many different windows of culture and language. My passion is to find ways that people can work together in a way that is imaginative and expressive to share their ideas, create a common vision and build a common feeling for each other.

Art lets people build up a common language, accessible to everyone involved in its making. Doing art together joins us as a team, as a circle, as a community of practice by helping us see and connect to each other by making something meaningful together. (The quilt on the facing page expresses the meaning a group of direct support workers find in their work.*)

Whether it's through art, music, or poetry, when people find ways to express their own vision by making something they have created a memory system that holds what they value and what they want. I'm deeply interested when one of the young people we work with in Brooklyn writes a rap song that expresses his vision for the future. I'm just as interested when people and their support workers make a scrapbook or me book or something three-dimensional or cover the wall of their room with images and symbols that have meaning for them. I'm not talking about professional artwork but about the ways people express the internal map that shows what they are reaching for in their lives.

The arts are the way we humans tell each other stories. Making art stimulates our imagination. Our work is about transforming and re-imagining possibilities for people with disabilities. Art gives us the media to practice that transformation, to try out different ways of expressing what matters to us and talk about the results in a way that brings it to life.

---

* To see more of Beth's images, visit www.capacityworks.com

Make Your Mark
Be an everyday hero

The hand print is a universal symbol of spiritual power, signifying action, strength, and protection. The hand prints found throughout time, in every culture, transmit the spiritual power of the person who has made their mark on the world. This image celebrates the often hidden contributions of direct support workers who hold the worlds of so many others in their hands.

Learn the Neighborhood

Beth Mount

Diana Whitney

What is Appreciative Inquiry?

There are a lot of ways to answer that question.* First, Appreciative Inquiry is a philosophy. It's a way of thinking about organizational change and human organizing. It is built on some very different premises from traditional practices of organization development. Second, Appreciative Inquiry is a methodology. It's a way to do transformation. It's a way to engage hundreds, thousands of people in change in their organizations and communities. And third Appreciative Inquiry is a part of a positive revolution, something that is happening in many different fields and disciplines around the world.

The definition that I use as my elevator speech is that Appreciative Inquiry is the study of what gives life, what energizes, what gives vitality to human endeavors, organizations, teams, people, relationships when we're at our best. Now Appreciative Inquiry doesn't say that we're always at our best. It does posit that if we want to learn and grow and make positive change in the world, the best way to do that is to study what works. Appreciative Inquiry says that inquiry is the intervention, that the questions we ask make a difference and the more positive our questions the more positive the information that we learn and the change that we create.

---

*Diana Whitney and Amanda Trosten-Bloom (2010). *The power of appreciative inquiry: A practical guide to positive change 2nd Edition*. San Francisco: Berrett-Koehler Publishers. Also visit www.positivechange.org

Philosophically, Appreciative Inquiry is based on the Theory of Social Construction of Reality, which comes out of a very wonderful little book called *The Social Construction of Reality*.* The field has been developed by Ken Gergen of the Taos Institute** and Swarthmore University. The basic assumption is that everything that we come to believe as true, as real, as meaningful gets created in human interaction and in conversation. So Appreciative Inquiry places emphasis on the language we use and the questions we ask.

We say that the questions we ask are fateful. Our questions determine what we find, what we learn, but they also create the realities of the world around us. Imagine that we are curious about stress in the workplace and we come in and we start asking questions about stress: "Tell me about a time when you've experienced stress in the workplace. What was that situation? What created the stress? Who else was involved? How did they contribute to the stress? How did you feel? How did it affect your performance?" I'm asking a series of questions that remind you of stressful times and prompt you to think about times that have been very uncomfortable. Though some would say these are neutral questions, they provoke your very physiology. Questions about stress trigger a stress response in your body. But it doesn't stop there. The moment you finish the interview you walk out in the hallway, get a cup of coffee and tell your colleague about your fascinating interview about stress. Soon you and your colleague are wondering why you still work in such an uncomfortable place. In focusing questions on stress, I've influenced what the person is thinking about, I've influenced the story they've told, I've influenced their physiology and the way they feel, I've influenced their relationship with their colleagues and with their organization.

Imagine instead that I ask about joyful productivity. Even as you hear the phrase, joyful productivity, you most likely feel a kind of joy. When I say to you, "Tell me about a time when you've experienced joyful productivity, fun at work, a time when you had fun and you got a lot done, and the results were amazing. Who

---

* Peter Berger and Thomas Luckmann (1967). *The social construction of reality: A treatise in the sociology of knowledge.* New York: Anchor.
** www.taosinstitute.net

was involved? What did you do? What made it so much fun and so productive?" That line of questions invites you to recall very different situations, invites you to feel differently, and gives you ideas for what you can do today and tomorrow to increase joyful productivity in your workplace. This has a ripple effect when you go out and see a friend and tell them about your interview, your thinking about joyful productivity, and now you've created a buzz. Everyone else in your organization is soon talking about joyful productivity.

Another way to think about Appreciative Inquiry is to go into the definitions of the two words. Look at the word appreciate and ask yourself or the dictionary what it means. We see definitions such as value, esteem, prize and to cherish that which we value. The word appreciate also has another kind of intriguing meaning: to go up in value, such as when we ask, "Has my house appreciated?" So the word appreciate is very strongly correlated to the notion of valuing.

It also works socially. If we give someone a compliment about the work they've done or a compliment about something they're wearing, they feel good inside of themselves and they reflect on that and it helps them to embody that value. So, to appreciate is to value.

Inquiry, if you were to think about the meaning of that word and look it up in the dictionary, you'd find that it means to investigate, to explore, to experiment and to be open to learning something new. So, while appreciative focuses us on the values that we hold, what it is that we want in our world, inquiry says let's learn about it and let's be open.

When we truly engage in Appreciative Inquiry we ask questions, we listen deeply and we're open to learn what the other person believes and thinks and feels.

This is very different from a situation in which I ask you a question and I really want to see if you know the answer that I'm already thinking about. That's not inquiry, that's a setup. Inquiry means that I truly care about what you might say and I want to hear your story and your thinking. When you put these two words together, appreciative inquiry, what you get is asking questions, being curious, exploring those things that we value.

Where did Appreciative Inquiry come from?

The roots of Appreciative Inquiry are at Case Western Reserve University, in the Weatherhead School of Management.[*] In the early 1980's professors Suresh Srivastva and Ron Fry and graduate students David Cooperrider and Frank Barrett were doing research in Organizational Development. They began to ask themselves how the questions they asked influenced the results of their research and did some experiments.

One team of graduate students went into an organization with deficit-based questions. They asked about the goals and the hopes of the organization but they really focused on what was preventing the achievement of those goals and identified the greatest problems. They learned about the organization through the lens of problem solving.

Another team of graduate students went into the very same organization with positive questions. They asked, "What are the greatest strengths of your organization? What is that gives you hope for the future? What brings you to work everyday?"

When the two groups presented their findings about the organization to each other they got into arguments as if they had been into two very different organizations, even as if they had been on two different planets. They recognized that the questions they asked were very clearly influencing what they were finding. Self-reflection also showed that the questions influenced how they felt about the organization that they had visited.

Some of the students who looked through the problem lens said, "No wonder people don't want to work there, it's awful. I'm not even sure I wanna be an organizational consultant." Other students, who looked through the appreciative lens, said, "The place is great, I'd be happy to work there. This is a great career path for me."

---

[*] For a portal that will connect you to the world of Appreciative Inquiry, visit http://appreciativeinquiry.case.edu/

They began to posit these ideas about human organizing from an appreciative lens. In 1985 David Cooperrider wrote his PhD, dissertation and first named Appreciative Inquiry.

Since then its been used in non-profit organizations and businesses around the world through the Global Excellence in Management Program. Workshops began to be offered through the Taos Institute, which I founded along with colleagues, Ken Gergen, Mary Gergen, David Cooperrider, Suresh Srivasta, Sheila McNamee and Harlene Anderson.

Tell us about Appreciative Inquiry as a methodology.

Over a number of years a methodology has unfolded. We call it the **4-D Process:** you begin by **Discovering** the organization at its best. You move to envision the future in a **Dream**. You then **Design** what it is that you want the organization to look like and move into **Destiny** or the realization of the dream and the design.

Because it is an inquiry-based process, Appreciative Inquiry always begins with a **Strategic Focus** that makes it clear what it is that we want more of in the organization and so what we will study. For example I've been working with a major academic health center whose leaders recognized that collaboration is a tremendous benefit at all levels in the health system and chose as their strategic focus "moving as one into the future". This notion of moving as one into the future is the overarching agenda for everything that they do using Appreciative Inquiry.

Once the strategic focus is clear, the next step is to choose **Topics** for your questions. It's a very important part of Appreciative Inquiry to choose affirmative, life-giving topics. These topics guide interviews, sometimes among hundreds or thousands of people, but the process is also important on a daily basis for managers and leaders.

For example, in healthcare, nursing turnover is a big issue which is frequently studied as a problem. The more we study nursing turnover the more we learn why nurses leave. What we don't understand is why they stay. When we're choosing affirmative topics we go through what we like to call the flip, from a problem, turnover, to why nurses stay. The flip focuses our study on those things that we value, those things that we want more of. As one organization put it, they wanted to explore a magnetic work environment. When we've chosen topics that say what we want and what we value, we launch those topics into discussion and into dialogue and then into action in the organization.

We turn the topics into questions and then, in a big organization, we engage hundreds of people in doing interviews. Appreciative Inquiry is implicitly a relational process. It's an opportunity for people who don't know each other but work together, who work in different departments, who may be customers and service providers, to come together in dialogue to learn about each other at their best. The outcome of those interviews is a map of the positive core of the organizations.

Discovery interviews focus on strengths, who are we at our best? We draw pictures –perhaps of a tree of life– that represents the organization at its best or we make a mind map that shows all of the positive images of who we are at our best.

The second phase of the Appreciative Inquiry 4-D Cycle is **Dream**. Many traditional organization development processes engage people in visioning and dreaming, What we have found is that when people do their dreaming after inquiry, their dreams are richer, their dreams are fuller, and they have confidence that they can fulfill their dreams. Because the discovery phase, which precedes the dream, is a time for people to really know who they are, to explore their strengths and to get renewed, when they come into the dream phase, they are bolder and more courageous in what they envision.

Another thing that happens which is great fun is that people are provoked to dream bigger by what they hear in interviews with their partners. A little voice inside says, if my partner can do that, so can I. If my partner can do that, so we can all do it. Building the dream phase upon the inquiry gives us bolder, more generative dreams.

We have found in almost 20 years of work that there are very few organizations today that are designed to liberate the human spirit. Most organizations today are built on the assumptions of the past and designed for command and control. And the thing that they most want to command and control is human energy, enthusiasm and spirit.

The Appreciative Inquiry **Design** phase is an opportunity to ask very important questions about the design of the organization or the community. It is a time to say what we have learned about who we are at our best, what we envision for our future, and what kind of organization needs to be put in place in order to support us being our best and realizing our dreams. We do that through a process of crafting provocative propositions, also called Design Principles. These principles help us to create organizations that tend to be more open, more collaborative, and more team centric in structure, in form and process than the older models of organization.

The fourth phase is **Destiny**, a time of moving into action toward the dreams.

The Destiny phase is always an interesting one because, even though we know that we see change beginning from the moment we change the questions we're asking in the organization, we are in many ways locked into impatience about getting beyond conversation into action. In the Destiny phase we often develop innovation teams which choose an area of innovation necessary to be redesigned if the organization is to realize its dream.

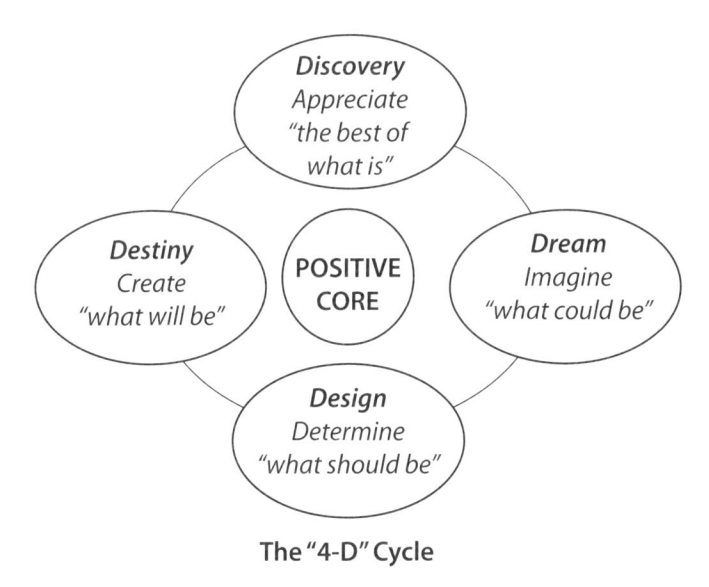

Discovery
Appreciate
"the best of what is"

Destiny
Create
"what will be"

POSITIVE CORE

Dream
Imagine
"what could be"

Design
Determine
"what should be"

The "4-D" Cycle

What are the core principles of Appreciative Inquiry?

Appreciative Inquiry is based on eight principles: the Constructionist Principle, the Simultaneity Principle, the Positive Principle, the Poetic Principle and the Anticipatory Principle, the Wholeness Principle, the Volunteer Principle, and the Enactment Principle.

The Constructionist Principle posits that reality is made in conversation, that all that we come to believe in is a conversational reality, that meaning gets created among people.

This principle asks us to really shift our thinking about communication. Old models of communication hold that an idea is something that gets formed in my mind and then, if I'm really good at it, I can put the idea into words and tell it to you, and, if you're really good at listening you'll get the exact same idea in your mind. The Constructionist Principle suggests that we make our meaning in relationship, that as we sit and talk I put an idea out and you supplement it and the meaning exists between and among us. Now, of course, we're always bringing the context of our past into every situation but the basic idea is that the words, the language and the questions we ask create the meaning that goes forward.

Because we are making meaning and creating realities in relationship, it's very important who's in the conversation. So, with Appreciative Inquiry we say everyone whose future it is needs to be in the conversation. My colleague, Marge Schiller, likes to say "Don't talk about me without me." This is very important because the old way was that those in power would make decisions for all of the people.

The Principle of Simultaneity says that the moment we ask a question change begins; inquiry is our intervention. The old model is that problem solving takes a long time. We have to understand the problem. We have to brainstorm alternatives. We have to do cost benefit analysis. We have to put together a plan. We have to implement it. We have to measure it. The Simultaneity Principle says, be mindful of your questions because words create worlds and, if you ask about what you want more of, those questions will help you bring what you value into life.

The Poetic Principle asks us to think about the metaphors that we use for human organizing. Many of our old metaphors lead us to think of human organizations as machines. If a machine part is broken, we throw it out and replace it. Inside the machine metaphor we treat people as if they're a cog in the wheel and if they don't fit in the way we want them to, we treat them as if they're disposable if we can't easily fix them.

The Poetic Principle says, wait a minute, let's use a metaphor that is more life-affirming. Let us think about human organizing as a story, as a text that we are reading and rereading. Every time we look again or ask a question, we're finding something different. In the organization, people are always saying,"What's going on around here? Why did they do that? What did she mean by that?"

Within organizations and within communities we're always seeking to interpret and make meaning, and so perhaps a better way of understanding organizations and communities is as a narrative rather than a machine. If we look at organizations as a text, then we can choose to study what it is that we want. We can study human strengths. We can study human joy and well-being rather than problems and deficits.

The Anticipatory Principle tells us that human learning and human action are linked into the images that we hold and the more positive our images, the more positive our potential.

The Positive Principle says that the more positive the questions we ask, the more positive and life-affirming the change that results.

The Wholeness Principle says that conversations are more effective when they include all of the stakeholders in the conversation. Getting everyone in the room together brings out the best of people. One reason that this is effective is that when the whole system is in the room you can know that you have resources and you can get commitment and make decisions.

The Volunteer Principle is based on the realization that people commit to what they help create. The more we treat people in communities and in organizations as valued volunteers, the more we tap into their own energy of choicefulness, the more they are engaged and the more they commit to what transpires.

The Enactment Principle encourages living now as if the reality you want is present. It ties into Gandhi's famous quote, "Be the change you want to see." This applies to the Appreciative Inquiry Process. We choose topics that really state what it is we want more of in the world. We choose peace not war. We choose to look forward to ways of working collaboratively not in conflict. Then we act as if that is our reality.

What has Appreciative Inquiry taught you about leadership?
We've observed four things about leaders who really embrace Appreciative Inquiry.[*]

The first thing we've noticed is that these leaders are willing to actively engage with people, and *with* is the key word. They are willing to sit at a table with others, and fully participate in dialogue..

The second thing that we've noticed is that these leaders are willing to learn and change through the process. They recognize that everyone, including them, needs to be a learner and everyone has to change the way they do things. Rick Pellett, the General Manager of Hunter Douglas, said, "I really thought that as we engaged in Appreciative Inquiry that many people in the organization would change. I didn't realize how much I would change and how glad I would be for what has transpired."

The third thing that we've noticed is that these leaders are absolutely committed to the positive in many different ways. They see an important part of their job as appreciating good work. They are committed to finding images of the future and affirming positive possibilities. They're committed to strengths. They act on what Peter Drucker said was a key task of leaders, "Helping people to know their strengths, to align their strengths and make weaknesses irrelevant."

The fourth thing we see is that these leaders care about people. Human welfare matters to them along with business welfare and planetary welfare.

---

[*] Diana Whitney, Amanda Trosten–Bloom, & Kae Rader (2010) *Appreciative leadership: Focusing on what works to drive winning performance and build a thriving organization.* New York:McGraw-Hill.

Noticing those four factors led us to collect stories about leadership and to do focus groups. Over and over again, people described positive leaders. Leaders with a positive attitude. Leaders whose language was positive and energizing. Leaders with visions that were helpful and hopeful and inspiring. Leaders who got positive results.

Our Appreciative Inquiry into leadership led us to define Appreciative Leadership. There are several aspects to the definition.

The first aspect of the definition is that Appreciative Leadership is a **relational process**. We don't talk about leadership as personal qualities, or traits or behaviors. We talk about the processes that happen when people come together.

Second, Appreciative Leadership is the **capacity to turn potential into positive power,** to see possibilities, to recognize strengths, to wonder about what might happen and realize it in ways that make a positive difference. Appreciative Leadership has appreciative eyes, it is able to see potential and bring it into effectiveness and make it powerful.

The third aspect of Appreciative Leadership is that it **creates upward spirals**. Upward spirals of energy, of enthusiasm and confidence that then lead people to make positive differences in the world that create ripples that magnify over time and across situations and organizations and communities.

So, Appreciative Leadership is a relational capacity that turns potential into power creating upward spirals of energy and enthusiasm and ripples of positive change.

What strategies implement Appreciative Leadership?

Appreciative Leadership organizes around five key strategies which can be carried out in a wide range of ways. I believe that there are many, many more practices yet to be uncovered.

The first strategy of Appreciative Leadership is using the **Power of Inquiry** and asking powerfully, positive questions. The second strategy of Appreciative Leadership is called the **Art of Illumination.** It's an invitation to see the strengths, to see the assets, to see the good. We want leaders to look into who we are at our best and reflect our strengths to us. We have a process called **Strength Spotting** in which we ask people to tell us a story that is a time of success for them, a time in which they were energized and at their best. As they tell us what they did we listen into the narrative to hear the strengths and we get to know each other through strengths rather than through problems.

The third strategy of Appreciative Leadership is **Inclusion**, bringing people together who might not otherwise be talking. In ancient Greece it was thought that when people come together the genius would appear. The genius, what my colleague Allen Briskin calls collective wisdom, shows up only when all of the stakeholders are there. We have a leadership practice called **Improbable Pairs**, which means inviting people who might not otherwise be in the conversation to be part of the dialogue.

The fourth Appreciative Leadership strategy is the **Courage of Inspiration**. People really do best, they perform best, they move toward change when they have hope. Hope is simply believing in the best in the midst of the worst. We can look around the world and see troubles and problems; the world is not the way I wish it would be right now. Appreciative Leadership helps people create visionary liveliness by inviting them to share their visions of a better world. It inspires people by appreciating who they are at their best and it gives hope by unleashing the creative spirit.

The fifth strategy of Appreciative Leadership is the **Path of Integrity**. We call it a path because it's something we have to do everyday. We have to stay on the path, but we also have to recognize and be easy on ourselves if we step off. Integrity means wholeness, it is connected to the root word for health. To have integrity means to take care of yourself, it means to live according to what is true to you, to what it is that you're called to do, it means to be true to your strengths and then to be true to other people, and to help them know their strengths. To help them be their best no matter who they are and how different they are from you because you see, the world needs all of us to be our best, and that's integrity, that's wholeness, when all of us can be at the table or at the playground feeling good about ourselves and each other.

So, Appreciative Leadership is a relational capacity that builds on inquiry, inclusion, illumination, inspiration and integrity.

Michael Smull

What inspires you?

What inspires me are the people who use our services, their incredible resilience, their incredible persistence. I've spent a lot of my career working with people the late Herb Lovett called "steadfast social critics". People who say with their behavior, "This is not acceptable. This is not okay." Who, when they are listened to, become people who actively contribute and are just delightful to be with. People who are willing to put up with our slow listening and our slow acting are heroes who should inspire all of us.

What drew you into your work?

Like some other people, I came into the work by accident during the Vietnam era. I graduated from college and went into the Peace Corps and after two years in the Peace Corps, I got drafted and was in the Army for two years. When I got out of the Army, I very badly wanted to work with humans; to do work that felt productive, that made a difference. The person whose couch I was sleeping on connected me with an agency that was working with people with disabilities and I was enthralled.

What are the origins of Essential Lifestyle Planning?[*]

In the late 1980's we were asked by folks in the State of Maryland if we could help get some people out of institutions. We went

---

[*] To learn more about Essential Lifestyle Planning visit www.elpnet.net and also read Michael Smull and Helen Sanderson, *Essential Lifestyle Planning for Everyone*. www.hsapress.co.uk/publications/books.aspx

into those institutions with the idea that we would do Personal Futures Plans with people.

We started asking people, "What's your dream? What would a good life be for you?" But these were people whose lives had been so terrible that their only dream was to live somewhere other than where they were. They knew they didn't like where they lived, but asking what their dream was didn't give an answer that we could act on, so we started looking at how we could put together a picture of who they were, how they could be supported and what life might look like then in those new conditions.

These were frequently people who were famous for the wrong reasons, people who were seen as being very challenging for the system. Quite a few of them were seen as, "Not ready for the community." Yet all of them, for the most part, successfully and happily lived in the community once we figured out how to support them.

We decided to start with an introduction that really makes sense for the person because they were already known for what they had done when they were very unhappy with what was going on in their lives, and most of what they'd done happened because of the circumstances they were in. So we began by saying what other people like and admire about them, things that someone would like to know to have this person be part of their life.

Next we talked about what's important to the person. What are the things that would make this person happy, content, fulfilled, satisfied? What just has to be present for the person to have a life?

Then we described what staff people need to know to work with this person. Many of these things were very simple. For one woman the core thing was always ask, never order. If you remembered that, she would do well. But if you ordered her to do something, she would go, "Oh, yeah?" and she could out escalate you.

With those simple things in place, we found that we could help people move to community settings that made sense for them, where they could grow, where they could become part of their communities. We found that quite a few people really couldn't tell us the dream when they started out of the institution, but once they had a life in the community, once things were going their way, then they could tell us more about what they wanted from life.

Is person-centered planning just for people with developmental disabilities?
That's a myth. The fact is good person-centered planning works with humans. We started with people with intellectual and developmental disabilities, including people who had significant mental health issues as well. Then we discovered that a number of trainers had older parents who needed assistance and they just naturally started doing plans with their parents, their grandparents, their aunts and their uncles. It works with people who have substance abuse issues and it works in family life. It works with humans. It's particularly valuable when somebody's lost control of their life or at risk of losing control and you want to help them have their own life back.

Are there circumstances in which you shouldn't do a plan?
If somebody has no one in their life that loves them, no one in their life that cares about them, no one in their life who's committed to them, then doing a plan with that person is unlikely to be successful and it's unlikely to be implemented. In that situation the most important question is, "How can I help this person have people in their life who care about them?"

If you're in a fear-based culture, a culture that's really rooted in blame, then plans may be done, but plans aren't implemented because it's not safe to learn. There is no such thing as error free learning, not when you're supporting humans. You're going to try things that won't work. You're going to try things that work. In both cases you should learn and change what you're doing based on the learning. If that's not possible, then you shouldn't be doing the plan.

How did the person-centered thinking skills develop?
One of the slides that I almost always put up during a lecture says, "A plan is not an outcome." One of the traps that we've gotten into is thinking that if we've written a good plan, we've actually accomplished something. The irony is that a really good plan that's not implemented is actually worse than a mediocre plan that's used. Because a plan is really a set of promises. A plan is a set of prom-

ises to deliver to the person what the plan describes. If you've created a good plan but you have no implementation, you've broken the promises. If you have an okay plan that you deliver on, you've kept your promises.

As people started learning about Essential Lifestyle Planning, it became popular and others wanted to learn how to do it. We started training people in North Carolina about what they needed to know to help people leave the institutions there. As it started to spread across the country we discovered that more and more people wanted to plan this way.

As more people learned to plan, we found that many people were getting better paper, not better lives. This was enormously disturbing. The whole reason for planning is to help people who are stuck find lives that make sense for them. And to see it creating better paper, but not changing people's lives was a true challenge for us.

We initially thought we needed to get better at teaching planning. We spent years trying to see how we could tweak the process, how we could improve the quality of the instruction and we could help people go deeper and understand what was behind the process. But over and over we found that we were mostly teaching people how to create better paper.

We finally decided that we had made a fundamental error. We were teaching a tiny percent of people how to write plans and ignoring the huge mass of people that need to be present and knowledgeable to implement plans. All of these people have to have many of the skills that people who write plans need, skills around listening, skills around discovering what's important to people, skills around determining how to best support people.

We looked at what kind of skills need to be present all around the person and we started calling that small skill set person-centered thinking skills. We started finding out how to teach those skills and discovered we could teach them separately from person-centered planning.

Now we look at person-centered planning as something that a small group of people need to know and we look at person-centered thinking as something that virtually everyone who touches a person needs to know.

How do person-centered thinking skills contribute to change in organizations and systems?[*]

Person-centered planning happens in a system.[*] Person-centered practices happen in a system. If people aren't thinking about the system they're going to find that typical practice doesn't move towards best practice. It is not okay for five people to have a great life and 5,000 to have a life in typical services that control and contain people. We want to move typical practice towards best practice. That's not about having a brilliant plan, it's about having pervasive person-centered practices that get reflected in plans. Plans will improve as practices improve.

Much of the what happens in services today is shaped by the fact that in 2010 most people are still living in group homes that would be very recognizable to somebody doing a tour in 1985. Most people are still going to workshops that don't look remarkably different than the workshops of 1987.

How do you begin to change this? Individual planning by itself is insufficient. We need to change how people think. We need to change how people behave and we need to change the underlying values. How do you change values? One of my favorite answers comes from a theorist named Burke who says, "If you want to teach values, start with behavior. Change people's behavior and you can change people's values." So we teach a small set of person-centered thinking skills. When person-centered thinking skills are implemented, you get person-centered practice.

Establishing person-centered practices goes beyond training. You can't simply send somebody to a course and then have them come back to the same environment and engage in the behaviors that you're looking for. People have to learn from practicing the skills, implementing the skills, and changing based on what they learned. An organization needs to be systematic in spreading

---

[*] To learn more, download Michael Smull, Mary Lou Bourne and Helen Sanderson (2009) *Becoming a person-centered system*. www.nasddds.org/Publications

the day to day use of the skills and provide opportunities to be coached and do coaching .

Once people begin implementing person-centered thinking tools they notice all sorts of simple changes that they can make within their current responsibilities as people who provide direct support or work as front-line managers. We call these Level One changes.

For example, we teach people the importance of honoring people's rituals. When anyone gets up in the morning they have their own way of getting ready. A woman I worked with in England is a "get up in the morning and be quiet" person. She lives with two people who are best described as chirpy. They get up in the morning and they're happy and bounce around. They're just delightful unless you're somebody who hates chirpy people in the morning. When this woman's morning was distressed she shared her displeasure, which ruined her day and others as well. Thinking about rituals helped them say, "We need to make sure that you have peace and quiet when you get up in the morning so you have opportunities to get ready at your own pace." This reduced her distress enough that her whole reputation changed.

Beyond Level One changes there's what we refer to as the coach's glass ceiling: important things that those close to people discover that they can't change. Incompatible people living together in conflict there's no way to fix unless somebody can move to a better arrangement. People going to day services that simply bore them to sleep and need something more productive to do with their lives. These situations require change that management has to pay attention to. They require changes in administrative practices, changes in business practices, changes in structure because they help services and supports be more responsive. We call these Level Two changes.

But there's a glass ceiling on Level Two changes. If you're busy making services are more responsive to the person and the inspector who does licensing comes in and says, "No, that doesn't meet our standards, that doesn't meet our criteria. You have to have these things present in the house, even though it means it's not a home", then what's required is system change. We call those Level Three changes.

We're finding that for Level Two and Level Three changes to occur, there needs to be a learning journey, a three piece feedback loop structured for change. We can't simply write a report that tells people about change. We have to help people go on a learning journey. We provide a structure where coaches tell stories and organizational and system leaders listen. Leaders hear, "What are the Level One changes?" What are the Level Two changes? What Level Three changes are needed?"

Please describe the person-centered thinking skills.[*]

The core person-centered thinking skill is sorting what is **Important To and Important For** a person and finding a balance between them. When we say something's important to a person we mean they are happy, content, fulfilled, satisfied and comforted. We have to recognize that what's important to a person can conflict with what is important for them. What makes a person happy might be in conflict with what makes them safe and healthy. What makes a person comfortable might be in conflict with them presenting themselves as a valued member of the community. If I was taking somebody out for a job interview and saw a spaghetti stain on their shirt, I'd say, "Let's find a clean shirt."

Finding the balance isn't necessarily easy. Just because something is important to you, doesn't mean you get it. Nobody has a hundred percent of what's important to them. Just because we identify something as important for you doesn't mean we should automatically do it to you. Balance comes when we discover ways that important to and important for interact. If exercise is important for you, what about exercising is important to you? Is there a kind of exercise you find pleasant? Would exercising with a buddy or a group of other people at a gym provide something important to you?

Dealing with conflicts between important to and important for by looking for balance gets away from some of the traps in talking about risk purely in terms of important for and forgetting to include important to. People who don't have what's important to them in their lives are frequently at greater risk. If all we focus on

---

[*] To download a mini-book of person-centered thinking skills, visit www.hsapress.co.uk/media/9852/hsaminibookusa.pdf

is important for, some people will complain bitterly about that with their behavior and increase their risk.

The better we understand what is important to you, the better we will be able to support you; so **Discovery Skills** are important. One of the perversions that we see is organization's turning **important to** into a paper form that staff fill out by making a list. To really find out what's important to you we need to have a conversation with you and the people around you and go deeper than just a superficial list.

To get a rounded picture, there are things that we ask those who really know and love the person rather than only asking the person themselves. We ask things like, "If you were suddenly going out of town and you just had two minutes to tell me the most important things I need to know to support this person, what would you tell me?"

We use the **Good Day, Bad Day** discovery tool to find out, "What's a good day like for you?" What's a bad like for you?"

We explore **Rituals and Routines**: morning rituals, rituals around going to bed, vacation rituals, rituals around spirituality, a whole set of rituals that are important to people. As we become a more diverse country we really need to understand rituals rooted in culture, especially when we're supporting people who can't tell us about their rituals, but grew up with them.

Then then there's a set of skills that we call the **Mindful Learning Skills**, ways to talk about where we are now. One of these skills is **What's Working and Not Working.** This is not new, Benjamin Franklin wrote about it, but it is critically important to adjusting to the way things change in a person's life.. An important part of this skill is talking about what's working and not working from multiple perspectives: person, family, and staff.

We've found progress notes that are useless. Notes that don't actually record learning but just show compliance: I was there, I did what I was supposed to do and the person was fine when I left. Most progress notes come in two flavors. There's the rubber stamp flavor: give me five rubber stamps, I can do eighty percent of your progress notes; and then there's the novelist. "As I was taking Michael out the door, the wind stirred the leaves. The scent of spring was in the air." But how can real learning be recorded? We worked with some people in Oregon and came up with the **Learning Log**. There's a trap here because the learning log is a skill masquerading as a form; so it turns into another empty progress note if people don't learn the skill of recording what they are learning.

When people get together to look at what they've accomplished, it's helpful to post **Four Plus One Questions** and have people answer them. "Since the last time we got together, what you tried? Since the last time we got together, what are you pleased about? What have you learned? What are you concerned about?" And then the plus one is, "Now, what are you going to do? What are the actions?"

The last set of skills are **Management Skills**, skills to create clarity about expectations. One, called **The Donut,** is taken from an English management philosopher, Charles Handy, who says that in all jobs there are core responsibilities, things you need to get right or else you get in trouble; then there are areas where we want you to use judgment and creativity and try things; then there are areas which are not your paid responsibility, so keep your nose out.

When people are in your life who are paid, who those people are makes an enormous difference in quality of life. If there's a **Good Match**, there's greater likelihood of relationship, and when there's a relationship, when I care, I'm going to help you stay not only happy, but safe. We have found that one of the most important things managers can do is pay attention to matches. We look at how your personality and the personality of the person match together. Are there shared common interests?

How do you respond to people who say that person-centered skills are too costly to implement?

I routinely hear, "We have neither the time nor the money to be person-centered." And I routinely tell people, "You don't have enough time and you don't have enough money to avoid being person-centered." Being person-centered is not about spending extra time, it's not about spending extra money. It's about using time differently in a way that is effective and efficient. It's about investing in the person, learning what's important to the person, investing in helping staff to avoid power struggles because they have the skills to have power-with rather than power-over the people they support. This means that people are serious about the day-to-day practice of person-centered skills, the skills that help sort out what's important to from important for. It's not just the form; it's the substance. It's the pieces that go underneath.

The 80/20 rule works. Twenty percent of the people that you work with take 80 percent of your time. Many of the people who are the most expensive to support are people who are complaining bitterly about their circumstances with their behavior. A typical system response is to throw staff at the issue rather than understanding, to try to contain the person, rather than support the person. What if there was a way in which those 20 percent could be happier, could be more content, could find their lives more fulfilling? Then time could be much better used in supporting people to have the lives they want.

How can we track development in the service system?[*]

One of the sad things that's happened in our work is that best practice, what we know we can do, has slowly diverged from typical practice. For example, employment should become expected practice. If you talk to people who are the best at helping people get jobs, they will tell you that the requirement for employment is twofold: a voluntary muscle movement and a desire to work. That's all it takes. But even though employment should happen and could happen and is happening in some places, it isn't typical practice.

I'll use an arrow to describe the move to best practice. The far left end of the arrow is labeled "Service Life", In **service life**, minimum system standards are met. People are healthy and safe, but people can be healthy and safe and miserable. If the system doesn't focus on what's important to as well as what's important for, then whether or not what's important to you is largely present depends on your luck. It depends on who your direct support person is at that moment.

---

[*] To learn more, download Michael Smull, Mary Lou Bourne and Helen Sanderson (2010) *Best practice, expected practice, and the challenge of scale*. www.nasddds.org/Publications

When systems focus on having both important to and important for present in people's lives, we refer to that as **a good paid life**. When we look at who's in your life, we see that the people closest to you are either paid or family or other people who use services. You may go out into the community, but you really don't have that web of relationships, that set of people who are looking out for you, who appreciate you, to whom you contribute in your life.

When people do have that web of relationships, they have what we refer to as community life. What we don't know how to do at this moment is to have everyone receiving services be at **community life**. We know that it's possible. We just don't know how to do it at scale. We do know how everybody could have a good paid life and it's not acceptable that most people don't, that most people are still between typical service life and good paid life.

Moving from Service Life to Community Life

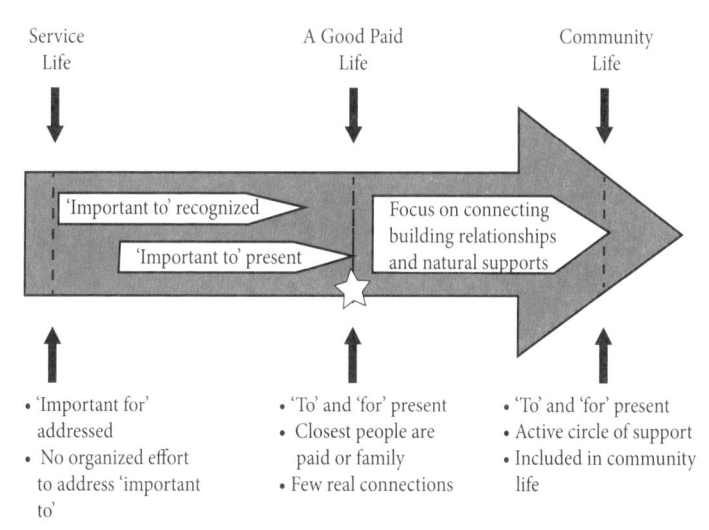

Service Life	A Good Paid Life	Community Life
'Important to' recognized →	'Important to' present →	Focus on connecting building relationships and natural supports →
• 'Important for' addressed • No organized effort to address 'important to'	• 'To' and 'for' present • Closest people are paid or family • Few real connections	• 'To' and 'for' present • Active circle of support • Included in community life

Celebrate Relationships

Beth Mount

Denise Bissonnette

Two years ago, I was asked to present a workshop titled "Beyond Barriers to Passion and Possibility". As I thought about how to help people see beyond their limitations and really take in their potential and their possibilities, I thought of the many roles we have to play. We have to be the dreamer and the gambler and the coach and the explorer. What came to me was a poem from the point of view of the people that we serve. This is what I believe they would say to us if they could.

Blue Skies

Pardon me, what's that you say,
"This interview is finished?"
Excuse me, but I've hardly spoken,
Don't leave me here diminished.
I'm so sorry to disappoint you,
To not have the problem you like to fix,
Instead I come with my own story,
With mystery in the mix.

You see, my hope is shallow, my fear is deep,
I have dreams I can barely dream,
But once in a while I can glimpse blue skies,
Just up the road it seems.
So, if you're the kind who likes to keep it simple,
Hey, I can handle that,
But please, don't pass me on
To another bureaucrat!

Is there anyone here who peers beyond,
Who looks behind the smile,
Cuz there's a lot about me you will not know
By opening up that file.

Is there anyone here who listens
In that rare and tender fashion,
Who'll catch the meaning between my words,
With the net of their compassion?

Is there anyone here who gardens,
Who tends the smallest of seeds,
Cuz sometimes I feel things growin' in me,
Beyond that list of needs!
Is there anyone here who's a gambler?
Who'll back a wounded horse?
Cuz I need someone with some faith in me
To set me on right course.

Is there anyone here who's a coach,
The one who loves that final lap,
Someone who will coax from me,
Resources hidden and untapped?

Is there anyone here who's a dreamer,
Who sees with faraway eyes,
Cuz my choices are looking rather dismal,
But I'm open to surprise!

Is there anyone here who's an explorer,
Who searches for truth beyond the facts,
Who'll focus on my possibilities
And not just what I lack?

Because you see, when I go home today
And my family asks, "How did it go down there?"
They're not just asking about my day,
They're pleading for me to report to them,
"Hey, I'm on my way –
Somewhere hopeful, somewhere new,
Just up ahead those skies are blue!"

So, if that's not you, that's okay,

I can handle that,
But please don't pass me on
To another bureaucrat!

So go ahead, scan the place,
Find the one who's on a mission,
To change the world, one life at a time,
Start with mine, you've my permission!

Cuz my hope is shallow, my fear is deep,
I have dreams I can barely dream,
But once in a while I can glimpse blue skies,
Just up the road it seems.
I don't need anyone totally brilliant,
Or particularly worldly or wise,
Just send me to that someone
Who believes in bright blue skies!

We are called to the holy work of helping people understand that space between who they are today, where they are today, and who they could be, where they could be, is the fertile ground that calls for imagination and creativity. It's the space where we question assumptions and explore ideas. It's the place that calls for incredible courage and incredible hope.

When people go into the world to work for the first time, they may be running low on hope and courage. In this difficult transition, we've got to show up and give people a vision of themselves that is much bigger than the one they see in the mirror. So creativity isn't an extra that we bring to the job, it is the very essence of what we do.

If I could make only one contribution to this field, it would be that people would bring the fierce powers of their imagination and their creativity to their work every day, seeing not only the potential and the possibility of the people that are in front of them, but their own as well and holding to a fierce belief in bright blue skies.

What is citizenship?

I believe what Native Americans believe: that every person born to this earth is born with gifts. It's totally impossible to be born without them. No one's birth was a mistake. We all come here with something to give. And it is in the giving that these gifts become medicine, for the world, for the tribe, for the family, the school, the agency. The health and the wholeness and the vitality of any community requires 100% participation of every member of that community.

Citizenship carries responsibility, "You have come with medicine the world greatly needs." This is a message that people with disabilities haven't heard much. Instead, it's all about, "What can we do for you? What do you need from us?" I like the idea of turning the table. "What do you have to give? Where you going to give it?"

I have worked with refugees and immigrants for years, so another thing that occurs to me when I think about citizenship is that at the point when they become citizens, there is a sense that "I'm not a visitor anymore. I'm native. This is my home." That's something we all want to feel in our communities and something we all have a right to.

What do you think has kept disabled people from the typical, everyday roles of citizenship?

Older people who have disabilities grew up at a time where we had a patronizing view. It wasn't necessarily based in bigotry or prejudice, but an attitude that, "We're going to take care of you." If you were raised without the expectation that you will participate, that may be something you never questioned.

I'm so happy that children with disabilities are being raised in a different world, a world that recognizes that we need the gifts they have to bring and that it is their birthright to be able to bring them.

What is leadership?

When I think of leadership, I think of Ghandi's tenet, "Be the change you wish to see". Leadership is often associated with a role or a status. But to me it's a quality that we all need to learn to bring to everyday situations. It's not the province of a fortunate few; it is the birthright of every human being. If we looked at all times in the course of a day, or a week when we are asked to make a choice, to pose a question, to advocate for a cause, we'd see many opportunities to show leadership.

What inspires you?
I love this world. We live in such a cool universe. I love the earth and the many lessons drawn from nature on how to be human. I'm inspired by people who have found their own voice; who see what they see and say it; people who like to live in color and are comfortable in their own skin. I like being around little children because that comes naturally to them. I love being around elders because, at the end of life, we're often very authentic. It's that time in between that we have to learn how "to be". I'm inspired by people who have found their gifts and a way to give them to the world whether or not it's through paid employment. Seeing self-expression in its many forms inspires me.

How can people make a positive difference in the lives of those who use disability services?
The deep work that people who work in this field do is to acknowledge the person inside the client. They're not a consumer or a participant. They are a human being with a whole life and a lot to give and a lot of opinions and personality. We need to meet people there, in their humanity, as people first. To dignify people and to treat them with the respect that they deserve has more to do with what we have to offer as people than it does with the services themselves. It's the spirit of the service that's everything. People know the difference.

I think there's incredible opportunity for every person who works in this field to use their influence to effect the work that we do, because it's all about connections in real community. People think they are their job descriptions: "I'm the job developer", or "I'm the manager". When we think that way, we don't bring all of the resources we have to the office because it's not on our job description. We have many resources because we're all connected, we're all part of a larger web. When we get out of the thinking that we are only our job description and realize that we live in a world with incredible potential for connection, we start seeing connections where we haven't noticed them before. The person coming for service has a circle of connections too. It's the overlapping of circles where change happens.

What is community?

Community comes about when people find unity from what they have in common. You can be in a neighborhood where there is no community because simply living on the same block hasn't given cause for you and your neighbors to gather. You can have community within a workplace or a choir or a book club because some common purpose holds you together. Community is unity through commonality.

How does somebody actually build community?

Community building begins with grounding people in what it is that brings them together, whatever that common purpose or those values are, and then very consciously acknowledging the importance of each person's presence. Everyone needs to feel, "My presence here is precious. I actually matter. I have a voice." There needs to be some deep investment by every member in the actual building of the community. Community building entails people taking the time to define for themselves what their community is, what rights and responsibilities come with it.

We're all born with natural gifts, something unique to give that's as natural to us as flight is to the bird. We can't not use these gifts without doing terrible damage to our own humanity. The healthiest communities treat as one of their greatest challenges to unearth the natural gifts of each member so that the whole can be bigger than the sum of the parts.

What does work mean to you?

Work is one of my favorite words and it is my favorite form of play. Maybe it's because I have found work that brings me so much joy. Everybody works, whether or not they're ever paid to do it. There's this bizarre concept in our culture that if you're not paid it doesn't really count as work. We don't do this in nature. We wouldn't say "Look at that little unemployed squirrel, that little unemployed dolphin." We would know that every creature in its natural habitat is working with everything in its nature to be what it is. Every human being has been working their entire lives to be who they are in their natural habitat; that work is part of the nature of existence. When you can find that element of play, that's when the magic happens.

What impact has the ADA had on the working life of people with disabilities?

I wish so much that I could say the ADA has really increased the opportunities for people disabilities. I do not believe it has. I think it has made employers a little more reticent to open doors because now these people have a right to sue. The law is there to prevent discrimination but the spirit was lost. When other job developers ask if they should talk to employers about the ADA when they see signs of discrimination, I say, "No way" because I don't think that opens doors, it closes them.

I think we have to open doors with other kinds of motivators rather than with threats. "You can't not hire me because I have a disability." That's not going to open employers arms and lead them to say, "Hey, come join our team." What's going to open doors is skills, what a person is really good at, "He's a kick-ass engineer." "She's an awesome secretary."

In order to really respond to the needs of businesses, we need to be thinking of employment through the employers perspective. They're not interested in good job-seekers. They're looking for good employees.

What do you see as the major distinctions between traditional job placement and true job development?

I believe the questions we choose to ask on a daily basis shape our destiny as clearly as the skeleton shapes the body. Questions are like the lens on the camera of the mind that tell us what to focus on.

In traditional job placement, the big questions are "What's the world out there looking for and how do we make these people look like that?" "What's the labor market doing? What are employers telling us they need? How do we take these people and somehow place them in those positions?"

Working with people who have multiple barriers to employment, I realized that job placement has a contribution to make but it can't be the only game in town. So I started asking different questions of the people in front of me. Rather than ask about their past experience and then seeing how that might fit with job leads coming into the office, I began asking questions like these:

- When do you know you are in your element?
- In what kind of situations do you feel like you are showing your truest colors?
- In everything you've done and learned throughout your life, what's your favorite problem to solve?"

And then we look at the world to see who has that problem and doesn't know it yet.

Job development works on a different continuum from job placement. Rather than trying to fit people into identified jobs we ask,

- What are this person's gifts and who in the world can really benefit from them?
- Where would these gifts make a profit?
- Where would these gifts save money or expand customer base in some new way?
- Where would these gifts be a natural extension of what a business already does?

That's job development because what we're doing is actually developing employment opportunities.

The idea is that the world is not yet finished being created and there is nothing more flexible or malleable than a business. The very nature of business is to constantly change, shape and position itself for greater profit and benefit. So why look at the world as if our job were just to fit people into what's already there? Why not take the view of an entrepreneur? This is when we begin to realize that we are not just job developers, but we are business developers, we are community developers.

The question is not who hires people to do what these people can do, the question is, who doesn't yet hire people to do what these people can do who should? Suppose a guy says, "I want to be a custodian." In traditional job placement, you go to the newspaper under custodial services or you call on custodial companies and ask if they have an opening. A better question would be, "Who doesn't have a custodian who should? Where would that be a natural extension?" I might go to a moving company because it seems to me a natural extension to clean the space once the furniture is removed. This is a new way for the company to make money because that service might go for $30 or $40 an hour on the open market and I'm working with a guy that wants to make $13 an hour.

This requires job developers to rid themselves of the notion that the only way to enter the world of work is to go for positions that already exist and the idea that if employers haven't done something in the past they're probably not going to do it in the future. Here is my promise. When you start looking for the opportunities that are out there, you are going to see something everywhere you go.

Another way of distinguishing job placement from job development is in how we think. Traditional job placement thinks of employment from the scarcity mentality: there's not a lot to go around and a lot of people are competing for what little there is. We've got to grab our little piece and hold onto it with everything we've got. Oh, and we're not going to let anyone else in on how we got it. This way of looking at the work world makes people think, "Too much competition, too many people applying for the same jobs, no chance for me."

I want us to move into the abundant mentality of work, which goes like this: for any given member of my community, there is more opportunity than they could possibly take full advantage of in the course of one small lifetime.

What I did not say is that there will be more advertised openings for which any person will qualify. The operative word is opportunity, and that is the focus of true job development.

Why would an employer create or carve a position for someone when there are a hundred other applicants who will take the job as-is?

It is an investment in the employee. It does take time. And my experience is that it more than pays off.

Every employer's most basic need is to recruit the best person for the job. When we take the time to actually shape and carve a job to the employee's needs, interests, and abilities there is a much better chance of getting the highest level of productivity and longevity than just taking the next person in the line-up outside the door.

The awesome thing is once they've gone through the process of investing in an employee, they are more open to going through it again. It doesn't happen everywhere, easily. That's why we have to be persistent and know that we will find partnerships with employers who are ripe for the idea.

What do we need to keep in mind in order to keep true partnerships with employers?

My partner, Richard Pimentel, when asked to define job development, said, "A job developer is a bridge connecting people, many of whom are ready, willing, and wanting to work and employers who don't believe it." I love that definition because it recognizes that we're not necessarily the missing piece in people's puzzles. People have what they need to belong to their world. What we need to do is get employers to open the doors and give people the opportunity. That is the most sacred part of the work we do.

Partnership is what opens the doors. The definition of partnership is that both parties have things the other party needs and wants. A job developer that just says thanks and moves on after knocking on the door and hearing we're not hiring has too narrow a view of the possibilities for relationship with an employer.

Much more is possible if you go in and ask the employer for what you most would like and, if that can't be right now, then follow up with a myriad of other offers of partnership. There are many possibilities., For example, "We've just started a mentor project. We're taking people in industry and matching them with jobseekers with an interest. Might you have someone in your business to work with them?" Or, "Times are tough. Wouldn't this be a perfect time to take someone on as a volunteer; we've got people that just need exposure to great workplaces and you make that list. "Or, "We're taking people on tours of companies. Would you be willing to have four or five people come and learn how your business works?"

We need to open our imagination about all the ways an employer can partner with us. And, here's what's beautiful: they will learn who we are in the way that normal human relationships happen, by taking small steps. They learn about you: this person follows through; she actually answers our calls; she keeps her commitments. If we build the relationships, hiring will happen. We don't have to worry about impressing the business community. Just be curious and impressed with them and relationships happen.

Stereotypes may be an obstacle, but my experience is that when an employer hires a person with a disability and finds within a very short time that the disability becomes inconsequential, the employer begins to value the person for who they are, for the skills that they have. Then just the most amazing, dramatic changes happen. Nothing is more powerful to change stereotypes than exposure to real people.

What support is important for the person who wants to work?
A lot of employment programs put all their marbles in preparing great job-seekers. They take people through a job search class and teach them how to interview and network and put together great resumes and present themselves. But employers are not interested in good job-seekers, they want good employees. And, let's face it, a lot of the people we see are never going to be great at interviews, and that's okay because they're not getting hired to be interviewed. He's going to be a machine operator. She's going to be a housekeeper. He's going to be a data entry clerk. It's the day-to-day stuff on the job that matters for job success.

As programs, we need to invest our energies differently. Rather than simply equip people to look for work, we need to pay more attention to what will make them successful once they're there, skills that make a workplace sing. Skills like: how to speak up when there's a problem; how to be a great team player; how to bring your own sense of joy to the job rather than waiting on the job to bring you joy; how to think little pieces of progress rather than perfection.

How do you support people to develop those skills?
We've developed a process of activity based placement that's supported by a comprehensive library of activities that people can use to become active partners in job development. These tools can be used in many contexts, but there is special power when a group of people support one another in the process of building hope, strengthening their courage, gaining esteem, and actually taking responsibility for their job search.

The curriculum that takes people from exploring what they want from work to going out into the world to search for a job is called *Cultivating True Livelihood*. It lays out activities that move people through the many small steps of the transition that a job search represents in their lives.

Cultivating True Livelihood: Work in the 21st Century

Course 1, The Spirit to Work: Fostering Hope and Shifting Perspective An inspiring collection of motivational activities designed to enliven and direct the spirit of work seekers. Sections include: The Rewards of Working, Work as True Livelihood, and Fresh Perspectives.

Course 2, Knowing Thyself: Assets, Strengths and Choices Developed to engage the work seeker in a more playful spirit than traditional assessment instruments, this volume offers a gold mine of tools to help the work seeker uncover the array of skills, abilities, and other assets that they have to offer the work world. The activities offer wonderful tools for raising self-esteem, building group camaraderie, and setting goals tailored to the unique strengths of each work seeker! Sections include: Inspirations and Aspirations, Inside Your Treasure Chest, and Work Preferences.

Course 3, Personal Power: Responding to Challenges Rekindles the dampened spirits of discouraged work seekers and prepares them for the rocky terrain of the typical work search - empowers them with a positive and assertive approach to facing current and future challenges. Sections include: Building Self-Esteem, Overcoming Fear and Taking Risks, Developing Assertiveness, and Fostering Power Thinking.

Course 4, Work Search Planning: Laying the Groundwork in the New Millennium Chock full of information, tools and strategies to equip today's work seekers with the skills and attitudes necessary to make their way, not only in the short term, but into the future as they continue to cultivate their livelihoods - long after they have benefited from your services. Sections include: Changes in the World of Work, Looking at the Big Picture, Provisions for the Road, Developing a Work search Plan.

Course 5, Tools for the Journey: Proposals, Resumes and Correspondence Critical for work seekers who need to "get out of the box" in order to consider new and creative possibilities for putting their skills to work! Sections include: Creating Your Own Opportunities, Resumes reviewed, and Writing Winning Correspondence.

Course 6, Researching Options and Opportunities Turns even the most passive work seeker into an inquisitive and assertive investigator of work opportunities in their communities and beyond! Sections include: Introduction to Employment Research, Targeting Work Opportunities, and Networking and Informational Interviewing.

Course 7: Contacting Employers: Takin' it to the Streets A wellspring of ideas, tools, strategies and guidelines for initiating and maintaining communication with employers. Sections include: Employers Up Close, Telephoning employers, Street Smarts.

Course 8: Interviewing with Ease: Mastering the Art of Self-Presentation This course fosters a proactive, self-marketing approach to interviewing and equips work seekers with the qualities, attitudes and skills needed to meet employers with calm and confidence. Sections include: Introduction to Interviewing, Preparing for an Interview, and Following Up the Interview.

For more information, visit www.diversityworld.com/Denise_Bissonette/publications.htm

Can you give us a feel for the curriculum?

Okay. I'll just say a little bit about what's in two of the eight courses.

Course Number Two is one of my personal favorites. It's about knowing thyself –looking at uncovering assets and preferences and gifts. One of the pillars of my work is a perspective from Buckminster Fuller, who once said, "Everyone is a genius in the right context". Everyone, just as they are right now, has the total potential for genius; our job is to find the context in which they can shine. We're not trying to create potential in people. What we're doing is creating context for the gifts they already have.

Many people come to us saying, "I'll do whatever, I'll take anything." We know that's not true, they don't want just anything. But, often people don't know what their gifts are, so, I lead them into some simple inquiries. My favorite is, "What do you love?" What we love is what we're here to give the world. What we love is what we're disciples of, what we're disciplined in. (Disciple and discipline come from the same root word.) And you know what's so beautiful? People know what they love. People know what they care about. They don't have to have worked before. They don't have to have a degree.

Instead of using direct questions, I use a variety of prompts like these:
- I know I'm in my element when…
- In the same way the bird knows it must fly, I know that I am here to…
- If I were to receive some kind of award, it would probably have to be for my…

- I'm always happy when…
- In the same way, you better not interrupt Michelangelo when he's sculpting, you better not interrupt me when I am…

What I have found is that people respond to different language. Ask, "What are your top ten skills?" and many people will say, "I don't have any skills." However, those same people will find their way to identifying their skills given prompts like,

- I've always had a knack for…
- My friends and my family have always told me that I am…

In Course Number Three I take on the topic of barriers. We love talking about gifts and dreams and motivation, but we don't often have a real conversation about the fear that going to work brings up. I think fear has gotten a really bad rap in our culture. We don't want to talk about it. We don't want to smell it. We don't want to name it. But, to me, fear is a kind of intelligence. It's a map that tells you where you've been, where you never want to go again. This is important information, but we've learned from when we were like five or six years old to just fold that map up and put it deep in our pockets and walk around like we're not afraid of anything. But when we ignore our fear, it grows. It's important to have a place where can take out your map and say. "Okay, I want to show you what's totally freaking me out about this whole situation." When you name it and you frame it, you can bring it under control.

Where people acknowledge fear they can find courage and really gain self-esteem by noticing all the ways in their life that they have shown up and responded to fearful circumstances in ways that recovered their dignity or their health. What I'm talking about is getting to the person's spirit. And, trust me, I have taken a lot of flack through the years. Some people say, "Oh, Denise, we can't be worrying about spirit. We're working with people with real problems: drug addiction, homelessness, profound disability. We don't have time for this spirit stuff." And, my question is, "Where else would you start?"

We've all had circumstances in our life that landed us on the ground. And, one way or another, we picked ourselves up, partly because perhaps, we had resources or training or support. But, I think it was the element of our spirit, knowing we're bigger than the circumstances, that got us back on our feet. I want to remind people of all the ways they've been strong their entire lives because courage doesn't come from some vision of what we can someday be, it is based in who we have been. So its not just talking about disability or barriers on the surface, but digging for the story within the story by asking questions like these about frightening times.

- How has this made you strong?
- What have you learned through this?
- What has this brought you that you never would have had without this situation?

What does it take to sustain us in this work?

I've spoken to the need to foster hope and spirit in people who are looking for work. This is a poem I wrote about taking care of our own spirits.

Rekindle the Flame
I see how you are all looking at me -
searching for that picture of purpose and passion
that I was when I first took this the job.
To tell you the truth, I haven't seen her around for a
while myself.
Yet, sometimes, I feel some stirring.
Something warm and glowing,
like a small, barely flickering fire in some corner of my
heart.
And I believe, if we could rekindle that flame,
purpose, passion and possibility could be mine again!

But it's not about having a daytimer.
I know we have a new time management system –
complete with the daily calendar, the priority stickers,
and varying colored in-boxes.
Those tools can be very helpful, I suppose.

*But perhaps if you could remind me of the seeds we are sowing,
of the horizon we are heading for,
Rekindle that flame and I will see my time as the precious resource it is.
My time here will be spent in sacrament, not sacrifice.
But it's really not about having a new daytimer.*

*I hate to say it, but it's not about technology either.
I appreciate all the new tools – I've got my pager, my cell phone –
Hey, we've just upgraded our software.
We're networked, we're happenin'!
But perhaps if you could you remind me
how the work we're doing with these tools
is somehow holy, or even wholesome?
Rekindle that flame and I could play a simple blade of grass
like a fine tuned instrument.
With a simple yellow pad and a No.2 pencil,
I will write you a report that will drop you to your knees.
But it's really not about the tools.*

*Nor is it about information.
Not that I don't appreciate the investment
you've made in me through training.
 You know, Tactics for the Tired,
Options for the Overwhelmed,
Strategies for the Stressed,
The Five Steps to Fame and Fortune.
Really, my bag is packed with information –
the walls of my office are lined with new training manuals.
If only it were about information.
The truth is that I am so thirsty for wisdom.
Perhaps if you could remind me
of the truth and testimony of my own experience,
you know, that knowing that lies beneath the notetaking.*

*Rekindle that flame and I will be teachable again.
I will drink from your learning cup like a desert weary traveler.
But it's really not about amassing more information.
So of course you are wondering,
"How do we rekindle that barely flickering fire?"
Perhaps we could remind one another of our collective purpose!
In a day of valuing diversity,
Could we focus less on what makes each one of us different
and focus a little bit more on what makes each one of us unique!
In this day of the contingent workforce,
Could we simply notice what it is about one another's presence
that is unrepeatable, irreplaceable, and totally worthy of respect.
Because really, we all just want to be one twig,
one branch, in some greater bonfire.*

*And if all of us could use our daily work
as kindling for the fire in our individual hearts,
the collective sigh we would sound
at the end of a very long day
would resonate like song
that would make the angels weep.
Let's rekindle that flame.*

Let us rekindle that flame!

Raise Expectations

Beth Mount

Jack Pearpoint

What have been some of the important influences on your work?

The key influences in my development are people from the margins. I've had the privilege of learning from people in villages all over Africa and India who have a relationship to their humanity that's powerful and beautiful. Their poverty is economic. Their real riches are in their capacity to notice gifts and build community.

I have learned from people whose life experience is radically different from mine; people who introduced me to ways of thinking and appreciating that I would never have imagined if I had not been their partner in work that mattered to them. People like Tony McGilvary, who spent 24 years in prison and then created a remarkably successful way to assist people leaving prisons to find jobs.* People like Charlie Tann, who after 27 years in prison was told he had only a few months to live and spent the time he had left (which turned from months into five years) reaching out to kids the correction system had given up on. Charlie's purpose, forged in his own life experience, was to give each of these young people at least five minutes of his unqualified love.

---

* Read the story of Tony's life and the HELP Program: Tony McGilvary and Marlene Webber (1988) *Square John: A true story*. Toronto: University of Toronto Press.

What does it mean to be person-centered?

It's about focus on and with a person. That is such a simple and elegant idea and tragically it is uncommon in practice. We're pretty good at doing stuff for people and about people and around people and under people. But it's not all that often that we pay attention and listen carefully enough to be with a person so that we hear and see gifts and capacities that are ready to bloom if they are nurtured.

What does person-centered planning have to do with people's disabilities?

I never thought that this work was about disability because it applies to anyone who has been told over and over, in many different ways, "You're nobody, you're nothing, you have no capacities, you have no gifts, you don't belong." The development of person-centered planning is a search for ways to say, "Yes, you do have gifts and we're going to help you and others notice them."

Person-centered planning is creating a safe place for people to tell their story so that we can listen and help those incredible capacities bubble forth and grow.

It can be for anybody, but it's important for people who have been particularly ignored because they have had a disability label put on them. The experience of person-centered planning helps people, their families, community members and people in support roles notice that their lives are full of capacities and possibilities. When people see their gifts and possibilities they are often ready to go for their dreams of full citizenship and others are often ready to support them.

Tell us about your early involvement with person-centered approaches.

I was President of Frontier College, deeply engaged with literacy and marginalized people: people just coming out of jail, First Nations people, kids on the street, homeless people –lots of people excluded because of reading and writing difficulties. Marsha Forest[*], my life partner and wife, was involved with this work and also with including kids with disabilities in school.

---
[*] Marsha died, far too soon, in 2000.

In all these situations we were trying to figure out what to do to see and show the gift in these people. Gifts are perfectly obvious if you look at the person one way and definitely not if you look in other, more usual ways.

In the middle of all that work to change the world, a very strange thing happened. Judith Snow, a woman with a disability who worked with Marsha at York University, ended up in crisis through bits of bureaucratic nonsense in the nursing home she was stuck in. It was clear that she wouldn't survive unless somebody figured out some big changes. Together, out of the chaos, we invented what Judith later came to call the Joshua Committee. It began when Judith ended up at our house and we called about fourteen people around and asked ourselves, "What do we need to do by morning to provide Judith with what she needs to survive."

We had to make a decision. Are we just going to save the whole world or are we going to try and manage to keep Judith alive? We decided start with Judith and so circles of support began to evolve and spread. The circle was about acting outside the usual roles and boundaries. One result was that Judith became the first person in Canada to receive an individual budget for personal support.*

What was your first approach to person-centered planning?
These pieces –seeing the ways that people can bring their gifts, intentionally calling people together to make high-stakes changes with a person, and working beyond what most people thought was possible– came together in Marsha's work challenging schools to include kids with significant disabilities.

School systems were scared because the adults saw these little kids as huge file cabinets of medical records and big lists of problems. They thought that the other kids would be as scared as they were. We gave them another way to see the situation, one kid and one classroom at a time. Susie may use a wheelchair and she may not talk right now, but what we need to figure out is how she will

---

* Read the story in Jack Pearpoint (1995). *From behind the piano: The story of Judith Snow's unique circle of friends.* Toronto: Inclusion Press www.inclusion.com

belong to this Grade One class. MAPS began as a way for teachers and parents and students to come together with Susie to work out how she can be welcome and successful in her first weeks at school. From the first, MAPS was about crossing boundaries of exclusion and creating membership. Given a good chance, kids came through.[*]

MAPS was invented as an end run around the medical model that pre-defines capacity out of people and shows them as a mound of terrifying deficits. We were looking for a way that people would notice that Susie is a really cool kid. When other kids met her that way, as another kid, there was infinite potential because kids would start doing stuff together and some of them would get along and be friends. And some of those friendships last.

How does exclusion affect person-centered planning?

The experience of being excluded is deep down in your gut. It's powerful and destructive to heart and soul. When you feel exclusion you see few possibilities and no good directions for your life. When exclusion goes with being directly controlled by other people you feel and are powerless.

Our society spends obscene amounts on exclusion and control because we are caught in a cultural trap of fear of some people. We fear people and therefore we put them away. We put them away in prisons. We put them away on reserves. We put them away in segregated classrooms. We put them away in group homes. We dress it up with the illusion that we are taking good care of them when in fact, we're creating a plexiglass barrier that makes us feel safe. It's ironic that not only is putting people away wasteful and expensive, it's unsafe. In my experience, people who've been put away get pretty angry and they play that anger out. It's unsafe for the people who are put away, and it's really unsafe for the rest of us because exclusion generates violence.

This is a cultural reality. It's not going to be fixed by just tweaking a few little things. Person-centered planning is a way of doing the work of changing our culture of exclusion by making safe and

---

[*] John O'Brien & Marsha Forest (1988). *Action for inclusion: How to improve schools by welcoming children with special needs into regular classrooms.* Toronto: Inclusion Press. www,inclusion.com

welcoming spaces in which people can attend to how they can make a contribution –make a difference in the world.

How do you know person-centered planning is working?

If we get it right, people glow. We see and feel the person becoming who they are, who they can be. Getting together for the plan results in something happening that makes real connections. The person engages more with others as a full citizen of their community.

Actions that build connections aren't easy, and there are no guaranteed results, but when we're able to listen to one another at the level of heart and mind we can create relationships that nurture capacity.

Are there times when person-centered planning does not work?

When person-centered planning is mandated, it can easily get turned into yet another set of boxes to tick. When it is just one more requirement that staff have to meet, it has to do with system requirements rather than noticing, focusing on, and developing a person's capacities. A person's life is mounded with yet more paper, yet more procedures, but very little action focused on who they are and who they can be.

When planners don't get the point of taking action focused on capacities, they just put people through a set of steps labeled person-centered planning. That's a waste of time and potential.

If we're going to listen deeply for gifts and act on what we hear, we're going to have to literally shatter the box. If a service organization is serious about leadership in person-centered planning, staff will have time and support to be with people, and listen in a way that begins or continues the person's journey into the community where there will be engagement with other citizens. As community connections emerge, staff will be able to step back and provide just the assistance necessary to support the person's involvement. The capacity for staff to use their time and talents this way has to be designed into the organization.

What are the risks of person-centered planning?

Forcing person-centered planning on people just to comply with a system requirement is unacceptable.

Systems can set up the staff inside them to just go through the motions of listening with no way to make the kinds of organizational changes necessary to take action. This is not only disrespectful to the person, it also makes staff who can't listen and act into complicit hypocrites.

What is MAPS?[*]

MAPS is a process of gathering the people who know you and care about you in a safe place to listen to your story and affirm your gifts with commitments to action. A sequence of questions guides the listening and we create imagery together so people can see what they're saying and can literally be on the same page. There is a facilitator who guides the process and another facilitator who helps create the images.

Sometimes people have difficulty in communicating their own story, dream, and nightmare. They may count on others to help. We do our best to start with what the person wants to communicate and we stay clear about the difference between what a person says for themselves and what others are saying on their behalf.

Once people have been welcomed and made comfortable in the room, people say why it's important for them to be there. Then the person relates two or three key events from their past that bring them to today. Remarkably, whatever bubbles up from the person's history contributes to the process.

Next, we focus on finding an image from the person's dream, which we understand as indicating direction for their life.

It's not uncommon for people to say, 'Oh, I don't have a dream." That is never true. If everyone in the circle slows down and listens more carefully, inviting and welcoming the person's dreams, a

---

[*] MAPS and PATH have developed over the years and some readers may be familiar with earlier formats. For our current thinking, see John O'Brien, Jack Pearpoint, & Lynda Kahn (2010). *The PATH and MAPS Handbook: Person-centered ways to build community*. Toronto: Inclusion Press www.inclusion.com.

dream emerges. Dream time is in imagery, which is much deeper and more powerful than just words.

The next step is to acknowledge the person's nightmare. Dreams and nightmares are sort of point and counterpoint. We don't dwell on the nightmare. We simply acknowledge and honor it in the discussion and by asking the person to find an image to represent it on the paper.

We've discovered that when people tell their stories in this way their gifts become visible, to their listeners if not to them. MAPS shifts energy and direction at this point to allow others in the circle to notice, name and honor the person's gifts and capacities. Then we create a simple image that emerges and expresses a gift that the person can bring at this point in their life. For some people this will be a new and powerful experience because they will seldom, if ever, have been told how wonderful they are and how much what they have to offer matters.

Finally, we move into a discussion about what it will take for those gifts and capacities to be fully realized in community life. Where do these gifts and capacities matter? What would be necessary for these gifts to be given in those places? What action steps do we agree to take to get started on making the connections and arrangements necessary?

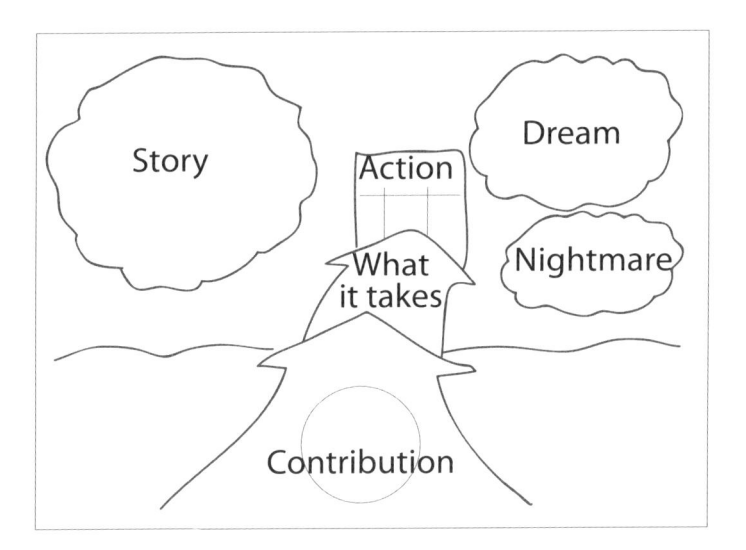

What is PATH and how is it different from MAPS?
PATH evolved later, from the complexities of work with MAPS. Sometimes what people need to bring their gifts to their community is straightforward to identify and easy to arrange, but sometimes people have to invent what they need to get where they want to go. They need to search for the way –the path- to a good future.

PATH starts by gathering people who know and care about a person, as MAPS does. PATH ends with the same question as MAPS does, "What are we going to do in the morning?" In between they are very different.

PATH starts by asking the person to find an image from the deep and powerful place inside themselves that holds their sense of their highest purpose, what matters most to them, their answer to the question, "What is the contribution that you are meant to give to the world?" We call this image the North Star because it gives direction by indicating a person's driving purpose.

This is often intense, but it's a search for an image that captures what is really important to the person not a complicated discussion that takes a lot of complex concepts. People don't need to juggle abstract words to generate amazing images with power well beyond any strings of words that we can put together.

The next step asks people to live in the future and describe how things look and sound and feel and smell after you have put in a year's hard work and had good luck and made real progress in the direction indicated by your North Star. The conditions are that whatever is described must be positive and possible. This is a time to invent the future.

The next move is to the present. We describe how things are now in relation to the positive and positive future. It's sort of a snapshot so people notice the tension, the stretch, between where I am now and where I want to be.

The *enrollment* step recognizes that moving toward the positive future from where we are now will take commitment. This is the moment to decide, "Do I really want this future enough to work for it?" It's also the moment to invite other people who are present to sign up to help you. Sometimes people say, "No, I'm not ready to do this yet." In that case, we're done for now. We'll come back and check in another day.

In *getting stronger* we acknowledge that there is work we need to do to move along the path. It might be to gather more allies; it might be to learn new skills or discover new knowledge; it might be doing things to take care of myself so I have the energy to stick with it; it might be following up on leads and contacts.

The final steps move toward action. We revisit the North Star and the description of a positive possible future. Then we identify bold steps in that direction, key changes that will take us closer to the future we want.

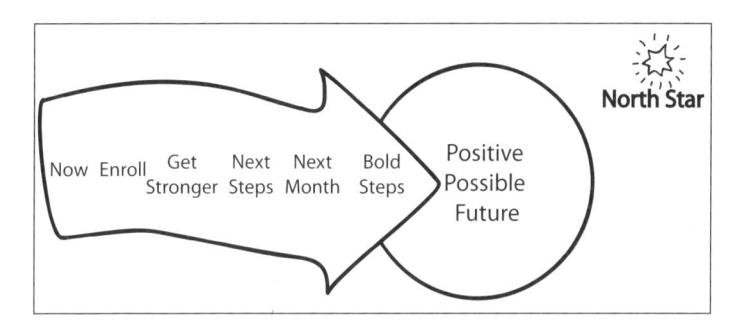

Now | Enroll | Get Stronger | Next Steps | Next Month | Bold Steps | Positive Possible Future → North Star

We continue to move toward specific agreements for action. What will progress on our bold steps look like a month from now? What are the very next things you are going to do to get progress underway? Who are you going to do those things with?

What's important in preparing for MAPS or PATH?

People need time and support to identify the people they want to be with them and invite those people. People who care about you. People who might know something about what you want to explore.

It's important to choose a good place to meet, a place where people can feel safe and comfortable. Hospitality matters, so its good to make a plan for making people welcome and involved.

How do you choose between MAPS and PATH?

If a person is at a crossroads in their life because a major shift has happened or is on the horizon, it may be a good time for MAPS. Shifts might be losses: a partner passes, a job is lost or left, health changes. Shifts might be opportunities: a new role opens up, there is a chance for a good job, an important milestone has been reached. When there are life changes, it may be time to ask, "Who am I now and what do I have to give?"

PATH makes sense when a person knows something about where they want to go but needs to figure out a way to get there because there is no obvious way.

The other important point is that these are pretty useful approaches when you need them. But sometimes the best planning tool is a blank sheet of paper and a conversation over a cup of coffee.

How do you address the concern that person-centered planning takes too long and costs too much?

We invest a lot of money and time doing stupid stuff that doesn't work because we didn't listen long enough or carefully enough in the first place. We can race around doing things that don't work and make people angry so we end up with behavior programs and other reactions that costs a lot and ends up with everyone losing.

Knowing and building on each person's gifts and moving in the direction that matters to a person keeps us from wasting energy fighting with each other.

How do we build community?

In our part of the world, we live in physical places but we are vastly separated from each other, so community seems like something lost. But there are people on the planet who do understand community because they've been doing it for a long time. We must listen to them and that's a stretch because lots of places that deeply understand the nature of community and how it works are places that we label underdeveloped. Actually they have thousands of years of development and there's profound learning possible if we would take the time to listen and learn.

When I think about building stronger communities, I have an unusual perspective. Many people seem to think that "we" have the skills to give people with disabilities a sense of community. What I notice is how deeply we've forgotten how to listen to one another. I see this missing listening as an opportunity for people with disability labels to be profound guides. There are people all around us, people who are marginalized in many ways, who insist by their very presence on slowing us down to listen more deeply. Then we can hear the gifts and capacities and skills we have to bring to each other. This makes them master teachers of how community grows.

Celebrate Community

Beth Mount

Mike Green

Where did Asset Based Community Development (ABCD) come from?

ABCD came from an inquiry about what local communities that are getting stronger are doing.* This included communities all around North America of every size and ethnicity. Some common ingredients came out of all these unique stories of what's happening as things are getting better. It's like asking a lot of people about their favorite cake –somebody might say carrot cake or chocolate cake or lemon cake– and then asking what all these different cakes have in common.

Three things were common to these stories.

First, communities that are getting stronger focus on assets more than needs. I think asset is a good word because in a business sense an asset finds value when it's put into action. It's a noun that invites itself to become a verb.

Second, communities that are getting stronger build relationships across differences so people who would not ordinarily meet get more connected to each other. Power, the ability to act effectively, comes out of relationships.

Third, communities that are getting stronger work in an inside out way, with residents at the center. This is more challenging

---

* For more about ABCD, read Mike Green (2008) A*BCD in action: When people care enough to act*. Toronto: Inclusion Press www.inclusion.com and John McKnight and Peter Block (2010). *The abundant community: Awakening the power of families and neighborhoods*. San Francisco: Berrett-Koehler Publishers and visit www.abundantcommunity.com/

than the first two findings because most helping and funding is organized so that outsiders control resources and decision making. A government agency or a foundation assesses what local communities need to do and then tries to influence them to do it. Our constant experience supports the opposite of outsider control. The more local people control resources and make decisions the more likely it is something good will happen.

Your work is in community organizing, what interests you about person-centered work?

I'm the father of Annie Green who is a 29 years old person with developmental disabilities, so my interest in the question of how people get the opportunity and support that they need to show up in a meaningful way in community isn't theoretical, it's from my own life. I resist the idea that you have to get ready to be a member of the community. It's contrary to common sense, and I know that some people will need well organized supports to make sure that their participation is not token but real.

The assumptions that the person labeled disabled is deficient and has nothing to give and that communities have no good reason to welcome their gifts is bull. I know there is a lot more basic goodness and a lot more desire for belonging to a strong community than we sometimes give each other credit for. This blind spot for capacity and goodness feeds the assumption that the wider world is always a threatening place. To overcome that belief, we simply have to get out more.

What we have to do is build bridges that excluded people can cross and deliver the assistance that each person needs to contribute. Many services aren't currently organized to serve a person's community membership, and changing that is what I think person-centered work is all about. It's the often difficult work of providing the assistance people need to connect, belong, and contribute.

What does citizenship mean to you?

You are a citizen where you are defined by your contribution, by what you create in the company of others, not by what you consume. All the strangers in our midst that are not defined by their contribution but by labels that lead to their separation are a great loss to us all. So are the people who define themselves primarily as consumers and keep their gifts to themselves. These are cultural problems. We get so many messages that promote consumerism that we might come to believe that if we're down in the dumps Oprah should know what to do about it rather than our neighbor or our friend ,or that we should go buy something if we want to be happy, or even if we want be patriotic and help the economy. We need to find ways for all of us to act together as citizens on the truth in Winston Churchill's statement, "We make a living by what we get, we make a life by what we give."

I think there's a kind of transformation that people labeled disabled can bring to a community that is able to notice their influence. One of my dreams is that the wider world of community development will recognize that when people like my daughter Annie are present, their participation is like yeast in the dough for building a community where we care for each other and really take seriously that we belong to each other.

Hasn't legislation like the American's with Disabilities Act made citizenship for people with disabilities a right and not an option?

Rights are very important and much benefit has come to people with disabilities by organizing around rights and organizing around making the service system more accountable towards those rights. But the move to community membership is through relationships, not through rights. Until I'm recognized through relationship as a member of the community who contributes, I'm not really a citizen. We have put much of our attention on organizing for rights and service system reform and that's very good. Now we need to balance that by putting more attention on community building and relationship building so people have full real lives.

How does ABCD compliment person-centered planning and practices?

ABCD has a vision of all people in a community being contributors. The foundation of this vision is the idea that everyone has gifts. The implication of this vision is that a strong community has a growing commitment that every gift be given.

Person-centered planning identifies an individual person's dream for their life and their gifts and then it asks what connections to the community provide opportunities to contribute those gifts. ABCD makes more visible where those opportunities might be and increases the chances that people who need them will find welcome and support.

In practical terms, I feel ABCD has until recently had a kind of blind spot about finding ways of integrating the personal assistance that some people need in order to contribute. ABCD will grow stronger by bringing together three practices: organizing communities to act on what matters, including an even wider range of differences among people as a source of power, and finding practical ways to be sure that people have the individualized assistance that people need to participate. The ABCD world has steadily grown better at organizing and connecting, but we've acted as if the whole realm of person-centered support is not really essential.

If we think about how people with disabilities cross the bridge from exclusion to contributing citizenship we can see ways to make both ABCD and person-centered practices stronger. ABCD needs to expand the practices of welcoming to reach out to people whose gifts have been hidden and people who want to offer person-centered support have to keep getting better at encouraging people to develop their gifts by participating. ABCD needs to support community associations to figure out what it will take for people who need accommodation or assistance to contribute and those who want to offer person-centered support have to develop ways to offer individualized assistance in the flow of active citizenship.

If Mike is a singer, he needs a connection to a place to sing that fits his sort of singing, say a choir. He may need accommodations to his disability and he might need a paid direct support worker. In addition to these individual things, it would be hugely valuable to have work at the community level that organized a group of choirs to grow stronger by becoming more inclusive. It's much more likely that people will have good lives as community members when all three practices show up in an integrated way:

community organizing, community connecting, and personalized assistance.

How does ABCD increase people's potential to experience citizenship?

We're not talking about citizenship in a legal sense. Every human being present in a place is a potential asset to that place. To the extent that any human being is alienated from contributing their gifts we have a collective problem.

The contribution that ABCD can make is to build a neighborhood culture where more and more people say, "I wonder what she could give? I wonder what that group has to offer." It comes to a kind of treasure hunt mentality, an active recognition that there is no one we don't need.

This is another perspective that ABCD shares with person-centered work: a focus on the half of the glass that is full. In the last century in Nova Scotia the Antagonish movement organized adult education and cooperatives of fisherman and farmers to take more control of their economic situation and their common life. Father Moses Coady, a priest who taught at St Francis Xavier University, was one of the key organizers and he said something that I feel is at the heart of ABCD work: "We will use what we have to secure what we have not."*

This is a different basis for action than many professionals use. Many efforts start with "needs assessments" that count up what's not there in a community. Funding often depends on how long the list of lacks and deficiencies and problems is. Plans get tied to filling up what's identified as lacking with outside resources.

For example, if we're working on violence, we typically want to know how many incidents of violence there are and what the police and gang workers and other violence specialists are not doing about it. This undercuts the inside out principle that characterizes successful community development because it leaves out the assets of the community and ignores how those assets could be organized to make the community safer. When you ask who in

---

* Learn how this work has grown and shapes community development efforts all over the world at www.coady.stfx.ca

this neighborhood can contribute to improving safety you find a lot more possible actors and many more possible actions.

It's like putting on different pairs of glasses. One pair shows you what's not there and you get busy trying to import solutions; the other shows you resources that are right in front of your face and you pay attention to how to connect them. You can't see what you are not looking for and some people are so invested in their deficiency glasses that they think that talk about assets is romantic and unrealistic. Those of us who act on what we see by looking at assets know how practical and powerful it is to build from what you have.

What assets should we be looking for in a community?

ABCD organizers think about six basic building blocks of community; each is a source of assets.

- Individuals and their gifts and capacities
- Voluntary associations and congregations, groups who come together around something they care about
- Institutions, government and non-profit, schools, libraries, parks, community centers, libraries, human services
- The local economy, the buying, selling, hiring, and investing that flows through a community
- The physical world, both built and natural
- Cultural identity, the history of the place, the values customs and vision of the people

To make those assets productive, it's necessary to understand two more things about a particular community: the web of relationships that connect people, and what people care about enough to act on.

What contribution does asset mapping make?

The reason to map a community's assets is to bring people who might not otherwise meet together to do something that they care about that won't otherwise get done. A lot of approaches to community mapping are more about data collection than they are an aid to relationship building and action. People can just go into a kind of asset festival mentality and count up everything then they

Community Assets Map

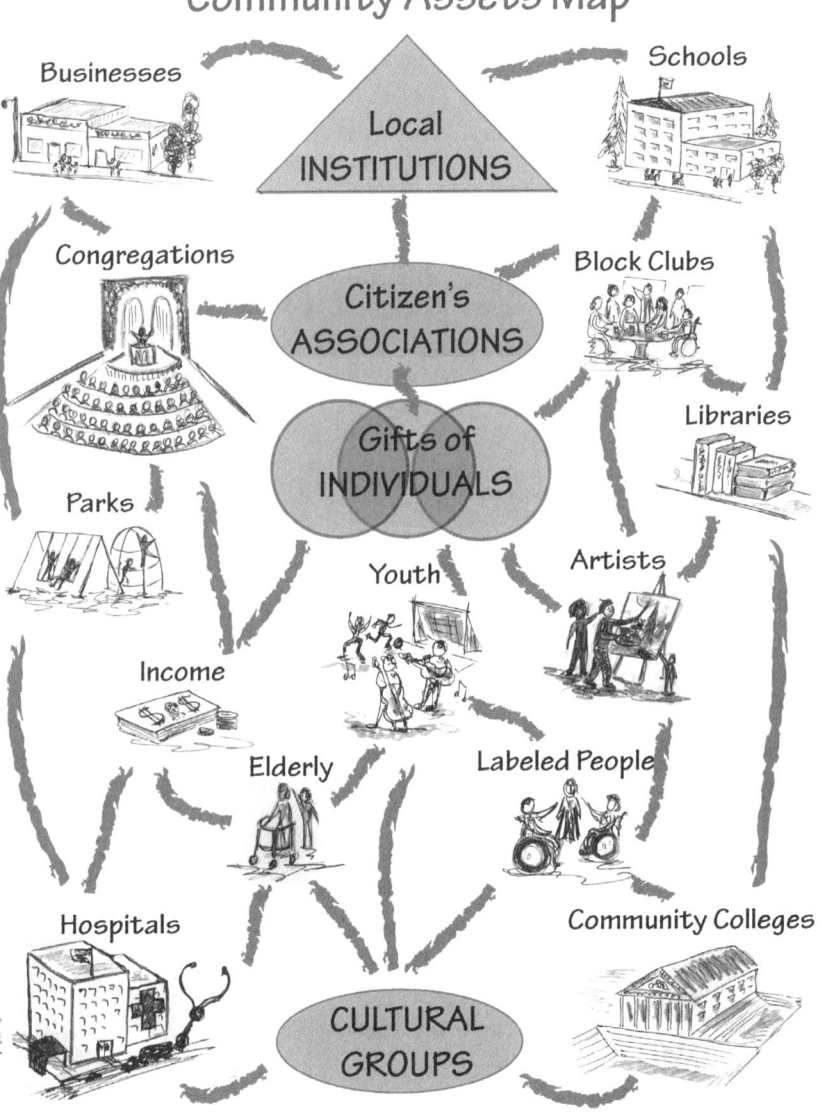

wonder what to do with it all, so having a focus and a purpose is important.

Sometimes it can be enough for a group to do a kind of asset brainstorming about the focus of their interest. Say it's a group in a rural community that wants to improve transportation for people without cars. They might spend half an hour identifying every local capacity they could think of in those six categories that might be connected to better transportation in any way. This simple experience of seeing their community differently can lead to new ways to connect the dots and find possibilities for action.

Shifting the way you see your community is a small thing in one sense but it can make profound difference, particularly in communities that see themselves as broken places. Seeing what they have to work with can lift people out of the fog of believing that they are needy, deficient, and unable to act for themselves. This opens the door to confidence that they know what needs to be done and they can do it.

What is a capacity inventory?

ABCD is a matter of finding assets, connecting assets and making assets productive. Asset mapping is a set of practices for making assets visible to a community so that the possibilities for connection show up. A capacity inventory focuses on the first building block; it refers to ways of making the individual gifts of people more visible to themselves and one another.

The most powerful way to inventory people's capacities and interests is through learning conversations. It creates a wonderful energy when people in a community are talking to each other about what their gifts are and what they might want to contribute.

It's also possible to survey people about their capacities. There are reasons to circulate written surveys but I'd say that the more people gather in living rooms or churches or coffee shops for one-to-one conversations about what they care about and what they can contribute, the more benefits there are.

We've learned that when many people declare their gifts it's like a crocus coming through the snow in the spring. It's a fragile, time sensitive offering. A frequent mistakes is to list a lot of gifts but not provide any immediate channels for those gifts to make a difference. It's much better to have a few conversations and then wonder how those gifts and talents might connect and do something simple and quick to make those assets productive. Further contacts and conversations will follow as the action unfolds.

Tell us about social networks.

In addition to their gifts and capacities, individuals bring their social networks –people they know and can call on in various ways. Social networks are one of two invisible drivers that move the more visible assets into action that addresses a community problem or a community dream. (What people care about enough to act is the other.) Every person has a social network that's either weaker or stronger, smaller or larger and every person has the possibility to have a stronger, larger social network.

Social networks are multipliers of influence. Think about it this way. Imagine that 25 people get together around something that they care about. If each person's network averages just 20 people that the others in the group don't know, the room is potentially connected to 500 people. If people are more conscious and more intentional about using their relationships, and particularly using their relationships in a coordinated way, they can multiply their possibilities for action.

Say more about the second building block of community, associational life.

Associations are voluntary groups of people who come together around something they care about, from addressing the most significant social issues to the most curiously interesting hobbies.

Many associations are informal like the supper club with no name through which my wife Carol has been involved with a group of other women for over ten years. Some are highly organized, like service clubs and religious congregations. One important thing about congregations is that they are usually an association of associations because there are generally lots of different groups within a congregation.

What is important from an ABCD point of view is that associations are already organized groups, so when you connect to an association you connect to an established set of relationships and resources.

What does it take to make connections between people with disabilities and community associations?

The most important practice is listening deeply, whether the person speaks or doesn't speak. It's also important that people who assist with community connecting enjoy making connections themselves and have a real passion for bringing people together. Many people who are great at direct support don't have what's needed to make new connections. When people are just assigned to make connections as part of their job description, without regard for their gift for relationship or their passion for community, it doesn't go well.

One of the treasures to discover in any community are the connectors, local people who just naturally reach out and find out what others have to offer and get great satisfaction out of bringing people who can help each other or enjoy each other together. These people are essential allies if we want to bring people into the action from the edge.

How can organizations become a real resource to their communities?

Organizations –institutions in the language of the ABCD building blocks– can make a critical contribution when they recognize that they can't be successful without a wider and deeper partnership with the community.

Schools are a great example. Very few principals or teachers in schools today would say that they can educate children without partnership with parents, with neighbors, with associations and businesses. It's in their self-interest to be more open and to see themselves as a treasure chest of resources for the community they serve. This means giving up the fortress mentality that makes them wall themselves off to protect what they have. It means joining citizens to figure out how their school's many assets can productively connect with community assets for the benefit of children.

Organizations that have public funding to serve people with disabilities have this responsibility to their community and another challenge as well. Too often the way they serve people with disabilities works against community. Service systems still put most of their resources into maintaining people at the outside edge of community. The basic question many human services have to take on is how to organize service resources as if community membership actually matters.

To find the way to integrate assistance into community life, we need more investment in practices that are centered on person-as-contributing-citizen. This means resisting the economic pressures to hunker down and focus on making things better for people at the margins of community. It means finding new partnerships on one hand with people with disabilities and their families and on the other hand with the communities that surround them.

One way to identify opportunities for community partnership is to ask what roles people with disabilities might play in making the neighborhoods they live in stronger and richer and what contribution the organization's resources could make to all the citizens who are active in those neighborhoods. I think it would be very significant if people with disabilities were to host neighborhood conversations, with whatever the right supports are. This would create amazing channels for people with disabilities to get in on the game.

I would love to see more investment in innovations that create living examples of participation and contribution. More investments that sustain connectors, organizers, and good person-centered support workers to purposefully partner with people with disabilities and their families to learn to build community. More investments in people who are relentless in their conviction that every person has contributions to make and that the absence of any of those gifts diminishes and weakens the whole community.

Listen With Heart

Beth Mount

Connie Ferrell

How does our society view people with disabilities?

Unfortunately, we're still in a place where for the most part, we see disability before we see a person, and so we bring a lot of prejudice and myth into what we see in a person. Many people have moved on from thinking "Those people make us uncomfortable, let's keep them out of sight" to "They can be here, but we shouldn't really expect much from them." I don't think these beliefs usually comes from an intention to harm, but sometimes the result is harmful.

It's harmful when people with disabilities don't have the opportunities and obligations of citizenship. I think that's because people, including some people with disabilities themselves, think that they don't have anything to contribute so we don't expect people with disabilities to have roles and responsibilities that encourage their contribution.

People with disabilities have made real progress, but we have to be careful of complacency in our expectations. If we sit back and talk about how much better things are, we lose the itch, the urge, the pressure that comes from saying, "This is better, but it's not true citizenship. It's not true inclusion yet."

We can see this plainly in the area of employment. More than two-thirds of people with disabilities are unemployed. This doesn't change until we expect that people will work and figure out what it takes for that to happen. As my friend Joe Marrone says, "To withhold the expectation of employment for people with disabilities is to deny them citizenship."

When we see people with disabilities only as needing others to take care of them, we rob them of something that is important at the very core of who we are: to feel needed, to feel wanted, to contribute.

What does it mean to belong to a community?
If you truly belong, you have these experiences:
- Being missed when you're not there.
- Having your gifts recognized and received.
- Knowing that your contribution is valued.
- Being in a position to welcome someone else into the community because you know that you are a part of that community.

How do staff make a positive difference in the lives of people with disabilities?
First, get rid of all of the myths about people with disabilities. Get rid of notions about how I'm supposed to act and be if I'm in this job role. Instead, be with the person. Really value getting to know the person and building a relationship. I don't think you can do much of value with and for a person if you don't take the time and invest the energy and the heart into getting to know them. Not just at the beginning, but more and more throughout the relationship. Trust comes from wanting to know someone, spending the time, taking the energy, creating the focus to truly get to know who they are and then in valuing who they are and being led by the person in how you would support them forward.

How do you see leadership?
I don't think leadership has to do with your job description, your ranking in an agency, or whether you have high profile in your community. I think anyone can be a good leader.

The people I look to for leadership have a vision and walk their talk. They are really clear in their own mind about who they are, where they're trying to go, and what they believe in. Because of that clarity, they lead other people. The best influence that a leader can have on me is to share their vision by living it versus talking about it. Every day, every minute, leaders demonstrate what they believe in.

When we think of ourselves as not being powerful enough to make change, we are really dead wrong, regardless of who we are. Every single one of us has an orbit of influence. Every day we influence things in a positive or negative way for people with disabilities, either intentionally or unintentionally.

Our power comes from intentional decisions about our own attitudes and behaviors. So it's important to think about basic questions:

- What is the change I'd like to see in our society?
- What's the change I'd like to see in potential employers for individuals with disabilities?

When we want to see something in others but we model something different, there's a disconnect. So how can I be what it is that I'd like to see.

What is supported employment?

I've been involved in supported employment delivery since 1981. From the beginning to this moment, supported employment is all about being still, being with an individual who has a disability and is trying to go to work, learning from them what's getting in the way, using creativity, problem solving, resources, to create a support structure specifically designed with that person to get those barriers out of the way.

Supported employment looks so different from person to person. I have certain expertise and knowledge of resources that I bring to the table, but the person is the expert on their life circumstances. So I have to come with a feeling of learning and a willingness to be guided by the person. Together we craft a plan for moving ahead into employment and how support is going to look.

For one person I may be right on that job, right alongside them for some period of time. For another, we may meet at the corner drugstore at the breaks. For another, some coaching and confidence building will get them out there and do for themselves what they need to do.

There are lots of rules and regulations that define supported employment as a funding source, but at its heart it is working with one person at a time and together making and following a totally customized plan to support that individual into employment.

The beauty of supported employment is that every situation is different and requires creativity. We can ask what it takes for this person to get and keep a job and then, as long as we stay within ethical and legal limits, we create whatever it takes.

It's not just individual circumstances that matter. Knowing and connecting with informal community resources is important too. Getting to work is a real problem when there is no public transportation and people don't drive. I was training supported employment staff in rural northern Indiana, where many Amish people live. When I asked about transportation problems, I was surprised when staff said they didn't have any transportation problems and I asked them if they limited their work to people who could drive. "No," they said, "we use Amish haulers." I had never heard of an Amish hauler, but it turns out that Amish people don't drive cars and in this area they have organized an informal network of people whom they can pay for a car ride when they need one. Connecting people into this network capitalizes on what's already there in the community. These resources may not be anything you can look up in a service directory, but if you go beyond the obvious when you learn about people's communities they are very often there.

What are the principles of effective supported employment?

First, follow a zero reject philosophy. The only criterion for being supported into employment is that you want to go to work.

Second, do a rapid job search. The longer the time people are engaged in assessments and preparatory activities, the lower their odds of getting to work.

Third, keep it person-centered. The person drives the plan and the process.

Fourth, include all those who play a part in the person's success in the process.

Fifth, develop one job for one person. Research shows that the individual placement model of supported employment is linked to decreased unemployment, higher wages, more hours worked, greater inclusion in community, and a decrease in mental health symptoms.

Sixth, continue the support that the person requires for as long as the person needs it. There is no time limit on the availability of support.

These principles serve an important purpose of supported employment: to create integrated workplaces, places that give everyone more experience of diversity, more opportunities to interact in ways that change attitudes about people with disabilities, and more chances for people with disabilities to contribute and earn.

How is a person-centered approach to people with disabilities different from other approaches?

I'd like to compare traditional services with a person-centered approach and insert a kind of hybrid that has unfortunately developed as service providers try to make the shift from traditional services to person-centered supports.

Traditional services are based on identifying people's needs for training and intervention. The focus is on the things a person doesn't do well, their deficits. Services are based on fitting the person into the program a provider offers that will do the best job of addressing the person's deficit areas and fixing what's wrong.

The problem with the traditional approach is that it doesn't take the individual into consideration. The programs available are the context for what people think about and do, not the life the person wants to lead. We all have things we don't do well, but in some cases we're not particularly interested in changing them. The traditional approach doesn't ask whether a person has any interest in developing the skills that would remediate particular "deficiencies". It doesn't ask what will move the person toward the life they want to lead.

The traditional approach assumes that the person will fit into one of the available program models. So the person is placed in the available program box that comes the closest to fitting needs. This hides an important sign that the traditional approach doesn't work: it takes people an incredibly long time to graduate out of those program boxes that are supposed to fix them and move them on.

Many people let us know behaviorally that the traditional approach doesn't work for them. Some people can handle being placed. Even though they may have square edges, they can tolerate being put into a round hole that they really don't comfortably fit. Other people aren't as flexible or forgiving and tell us that what we are doing isn't working, sometimes very dramatically with difficult behavior and sometimes by withdrawing. But the traditional approach makes these messages hard to understand; they are heard as symptoms of more deficits to fix in the person and not as demands to change the approach to better fit the way the person wants to live.

A person-centered approach is the opposite of the traditional approach. We look at the person and where they're trying to go with their lives. We ask,

- What are your talents and gifts?
- What skills and knowledge do you care about developing?
- What is a meaningful life from your perspective?
- If you could close your eyes and think about having a life that you'd really love to have five years from now, what would it look like?
    - Where would you be living?
    - What would you be doing?
    - Who would you be hanging out with?

Then coming backwards and asking:

- What's keeping that from happening?
- What do you have going for you?
- Why does this make sense in relationships to the who you are?
- What are the barriers?

Once we've explored those questions, we try to figure out how the person's natural support system, together with the human service system's resources, can help the person along their own life's path. We start from program amnesia. We forget the boxes of pre-voc or workshop and work on crafting something customized to fit each unique individual.

Then there's the third model, a hybrid of the first two, the customer-driven approach. It's sort of the Burger King idea: you can have it your way, but don't go crazy on us. We don't just put you in a program box based on our assessment of your deficiencies. You don't have to move through a continuum of placements to get to a job or a place to live. We consider your preferences. But it's not like the world is yours, we have a menu. We have a limited number of options and some flexibility, so we can modify what we have a bit. But we can't forget about our programs and customize supports to match you.

I don't want to put the customer driven approach down. It's better than the traditional approach. However, it will get in the way of moving to a person-centered approach if an organization stops there and thinks they've arrived. To keep developing, call the customer-driven approach what it is, be clear about the dramatic differences between a customer-driven approach and a person-centered approach, and develop strategies to keep moving on toward person-centeredness.

Traditional Approach	Customer Driven Approach	Person-Centered Approach
Analyze person's deficits, define needs and make a plan to fix what's wrong	Ask person to identify the needs they want to work on	Start with the person's ideals and value system
Fit person into best currently available service program	Make program options more flexible to allow for some choice	Customize supports and maximize community engagement

How do you see the difference between person-centered planning and person-centeredness?

Person-centered planning is certainly a part of person-centeredness, but it's not all that we're talking about. A lot of agencies have moved to person-centered planning and confuse that with embracing person-centeredness. That's not enough: person-centered planning without person-centered work is empty.

Good person-centered planning usually makes good things happen in the room where the plan gets made. We bring the players together, we start with positive attributes, we come up with a plan based on individual interests and abilities.

But if it's business is as usual as far as what we actually do with a person on a day-to-day basis, then how a person spends their time and where they're putting their precious efforts remains basically the same. We've create an expectation that things are going be different and they really aren't.

Person-centeredness is about really being with the person, visiting where they're trying to go with their lives, and truly committing yourself. It means developing the ability to pull together a team of people that reaches beyond our current programs and agencies. It means making our resources so flexible that we really can practice program amnesia and fit our support closely to the direction that each person wants their life to go.

What do we have to give up in order to move to person-centered work?

We get stuck sometimes because person-centered work is more about asking the right questions than giving the right answers. I think many of us who have been in this business for a long time were brought up to believe that we have a professional responsibility to come up with the answers and solve any problems that come up. It's part of the traditional assumption that services exist to fix the person and people can misunderstand being person-centered as taking full responsibility for delivering whatever the person wants.

We're really talking about a complete realignment of our professional role in the lives of people with disabilities. So as long as we hold on to the idea that we staff have total responsibility to make what the plan says happen, for fixing you or making your life work exactly the way you want it to work, we're going to create a menu of choices that's still very limited. Holding complete responsibility for fixing inevitably puts us in control of people's lives.

We need to make the shift to thinking of ourselves as listener, question asker, idea creator, facilitator, bridge builder. Our role is to help each person clarify their answers to these questions:
- What is it that I want in my life and from my life?
- Who are the right people to help me move towards your life goal?
- How can service resources help?

What is the Framework for Planning?

Carol Blessing and I were asked to provide training and facilitate a person-centered planning process with a man who was at risk of losing employment services because it appeared to the team that he wasn't motivated because he hadn't kept any of the several jobs that they had found for him.

Because we wanted to fully involve him in his planning process, we invited him to attend the training and then consult with us on what would suit him best. He said that planning should begin with an understanding of a person's core values and keep those values central to everything else. Based on his insight, we came up with A Framework for Planning as a container for information that comes from exploration and discovery.

The Framework guides an inquiry process for a purpose that's important to the person, for example "to find a direction for employment." It has eight sections, seven to focus the process of gather-

A Framework for Planning

Purpose:

- Attributes and Talents
- Interest, Experience, Skills and Hobbies
- Preferences and Priorities
- Values and Ideals
- Supports Needed or Desired
- Community Connections
- Resources and Networks
- Action Planning

©2006 Carol Blessing and Connie Ferrell

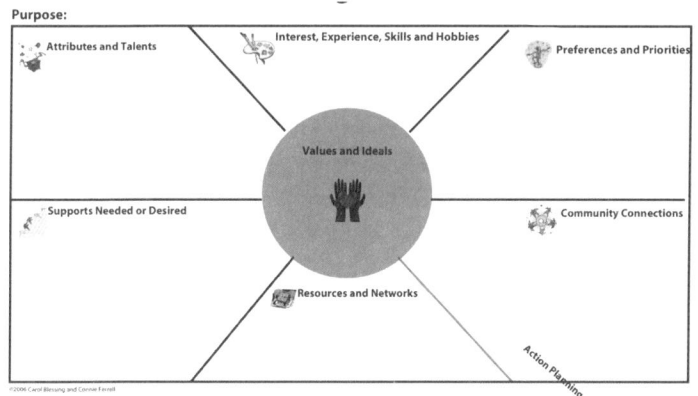

ing information and an action plan that synthesizes what's been discovered. The sections fit together to define a positive profile of the person and how they're trying to move ahead in their life. Three sections create an insider-view of who this person is, their abilities, interests, experiences and skills and their preferences and priorities related to the plan's purpose. Three sections identify the connections, networks, resources and supports the person can draw on or needs to develop. Energy grows when people begin to move outside what the service system can do and identify where in the world a person could be involved and included, belong and contribute.

As information begins to fill these six sections, the facilitator listens for and helps those involved in the process identify common themes that can be distilled into a statement of the person's core value. A core value is more than a person's next goal. It's a part of their identity that stays pretty similar throughout life. Once identified, this core value becomes the compass that guides everything from that point forward in planning and offering support. Actions that flow from a person's core value are likely to work.

A dream without an action plan is nothing but a frustration; so the eighth step identifies next steps that people take responsibility for doing. A good action plan pulls together all the information that has been shared and faces the person with a choice about what they are most interested in pursuing and what they are going to do next.

The Framework is structured to support a creative process that's based on listening comprehensively and organizing information in a way that leads to action that respects a person's core value and connects them more strongly to the world. It's not a list of specific questions that magically produce results. It's a reminder of what's worth inquiring about, a record of what matters to a person, and a guide for creatively turning information into action.*

---

* For more information on *The Framework for Planning* and to order materials, e-mail Integrated Services at Cferrell_connie@yahoo.com

John O'Brien

What is disability?

Disability is a social construction. In different contexts, there are different ways of understanding the kinds of human differences that require accommodation or assistance if a person is to have a good life. In the context of eligibility for social security payments or publicly funded services or protection under the ADA, it has criteria specified in law.

In the disabled people's movement, it has political meaning. Advocates for the social model of disability assert a critical distinction between impairment –differences in functioning that require accommodation or assistance– and disability –disadvantage that results from societal failures to do what is necessary to allow people with impairments a fair share of the benefits of citizenship. Others, for instance some people with autism, say that what others label as disability is simply another way of being fully human. All these understandings are the subject of continuing debate.

In this interview, when I say "people with disabilities" I'm thinking about people who require substantial amounts of assistance throughout their lives, assistance that is designed and delivered with deep attention to their individual circumstances and great imagination in figuring out how to discover and support the life they would value living. These are the people I met in dire institutional conditions more than forty years ago and the people I continue to have the privilege of learning with today.

Why is citizenship important for people with disabilities?
Citizens are people who can say, "I belong to this place and it's people and I'm able and willing to act from responsibility for my belonging." People with disabilities are among those who are vulnerable to social exclusion: being pushed to the edges of society and deprived of what they require to participate actively. Citizenship creates a framework for understanding what it is that we're really trying to do when we become allies with people with disabilities who are seeking a life that makes sense.

One way to think about it is to consider three dimensions of citizenship: legal, political and social. Starting in the 1960's, the legal benefits of citizenship began to come to people with disabilities as a growing number of citizens recoiled from the terrible conditions in institutions. The courts and legislatures have set limits on how people with disabilities can be treated and, to a lesser extent, have created duties of reasonable accommodation and reasonable progress toward alternatives to institutionalization (when it comes to people who are socially devalued the law is always "reasonable" in the duties it imposes on governments and businesses). In the same period, the political dimension of citizenship has expanded as more and more disabled people and their families have claimed the right to make decisions in their own lives and organized to influence law and policy.

The social dimension of citizenship recognizes that there's no way for a community to be healthy if its people aren't actively engaged in organizing themselves, defining the kinds of issues that allow their communities to thrive, and working together to make progress on those issues. On the other hand, there is no way that people can flourish without the fruits of this kind of healthy collective action around them.

All three dimensions of citizenship are contested. No law book or civics book or journal of evidence-based practice provides final answers to basic questions like where the limits of accommodation are or what supports people are entitled to as a matter of right. There is continuing conflict about the most important issues such as the role of institutions or the legitimacy of special schools. So citizenship is the space in which we keep struggling to understand what our freedom means in the presence of difference, and in particular in the presence of dependency (which I take to mean requiring significant amounts of extra help to make it through your day or week). People with disabilities are at an edge of a centuries long process of negotiating who really belongs to communities, who really is one of us, who really has a voice worth hearing and the power necessary to live as they value living in company with friends and allies.

Historically, humans haven't been that good at seeing citizenship in an inclusive way. Aristotle championed citizenship, but he could only imagine free Athenian men when he thought of it. The United States Constitution defined slaves as three-fifths of a person to make up the count that allocated representation and accorded them no rights. American women didn't get a federal right to vote until 1920. African American people continued to have trouble with the political dimension of citizenship well into the 1970's. People with disabilities are just beginning to have what they need to enact their citizenship, not just in the voting booth or the courthouse, but through the engagement in civic life that forms the social foundation for law and politics. Providing the support necessary for people who need it to engage the responsibilities of citizenship is a key reason for person-centered work.

What keeps people with disabilities from being full citizens with access to valued community roles?

At least three things would go on my list. First and obvious is inaccessibility. Until very recently, we didn't design our buildings, busses, or subways to be accessible. Physical accessibility is the most straightforward kind and we are, too slowly, catching up. But we are only beginning to learn how to enable active participation by people with intellectual disabilities, or the sensory and movement impairments that get labeled as autism, or the experiences that get labeled as chronic and persistent mental illness. Lack of appreciation of what people can accomplish with good assistance leads to pitifully low expectations for their development and stunts the invention of ways to support their full participation.

Second is fear of the sort of difference that people with disabilities represent to many people. Fear creates a negative sense of otherness that leads to avoidance if not active rejection. Ill formed fantasies of what it would be like to live in that body or to live with that mind can even bring people to think, "I'd rather be dead than be like that."

Third, as a society we are not very good at thinking about and responding to dependency. Myths of independence keep the work of caring –from child rearing to assisting incontinent elders– mostly invisible, socially devalued, poorly compensated, and mostly assigned to women, often women of color. Many people with disabilities raise the question of interdependence in human experience simply by showing up, and this can be uncomfortable. It probably explains why we tend to offer opportunities for employment and other ordinary experiences to those who seem most like "us" and appear "independent" –most able to manage without much assistance.

The hard news is that people with disabilities can respond to the prejudiced treatment that gets stacked on top of the consequences of whatever impairments they might experience by withdrawing from the possibility of participation in the workforce and in civic life. They may even internalize the social beliefs that devalue them and falsely justify their exclusion and come to see themselves as embodying shame or as lacking anything meaningful to contribute. So we create a world that divides around difference and dependency and a forgetting occurs: we don't know that people with disabilities are "us" and we imagine them as "them". And some people with disabilities may not remember that they belong either.

The good news is that, given the opportunity, so many people with disabilities reach through all this and connect to their fellow citizens in good ways that overcome fear, establish a fruitful interdependence, and make access and accommodation a straightforward matter. Person-centered work aims to assist people with disabilities in bending or slipping through the social rules of exclusion.

How does all this matter to person-centered work?

When I am wondering about why things aren't going as well as I think they should for people we partner and plan with, it helps me to think about the bigger picture we practice in and what gives us good odds at changing it. There is plenty to do beside person-centered work, but person-centered work is one condition for more people with disabilities doing the legal and political and civic work required to build more just and inclusive communities.

Our legal and political situation is full of contradictions which reflect the best current balance of competing interests. For example, the US signs the *UN Convention on the Rights of Persons with Disabilities*,* which affirms the rights of all people with disabilities to an integrated life, to support for employment, to inclusive education, to self-determination. The same administration budgets billions of dollars for nursing homes and institutions and maintains financial incentives to provide assistance and education in ways that segregate, impose control, and discourage employment. The point: person-centered work offers people the opportunity to jump into these contradictions and find ways to make the best of them; its practitioners can't expect a system whose commitments are uncompromised. Another point: those who want the benefits of person-centered work have the chance to exercise their political citizenship in support of a better settlement.

Our legal and political achievements are well ahead of our system's capacity to deliver. Hard political work has persuaded policy makers to adopt self-determination and person-centered individualized supports as central principles. But we don't yet know how to shift a system with most of its resources sunk in services that decide for people and manage them as members of groups. And there is much left to figure out about supporting self determination and supporting people in person-centered ways. Those who expect a person-centered plan to lead smoothly into easily directed supports set a course for disappointment and even cynicism. Anyone who thinks these are just problems of implementation that can be solved with clever management fixes underestimates the depth of the trouble. The name of the real game is social innovation: designing new ways to learn with people how to support a life that matters to them. This isn't a matter of meeting consumer needs or delighting customers. In fact thinking of people as consumers misdirects attention from the question of

---
* http://www.un.org/disabilities

encouraging and supporting active citizenship. Person-centered work is about engaging people in leadership.

What is leadership?

When changes have come for people with disabilities, it's because people come to awareness that unless we're willing to generate power with people and invent new forms of support, circumstances that are unacceptable by any common sense of decency will perpetuate themselves.

Most service organizations have the social function of putting people to sleep, keeping them from seeing the social reality that faces people with disabilities. This function mostly conceals itself from those who perform it. People go to sleep when the slogan that "we are doing the best that is possible for 'them'" distracts from noticing and taking responsibility for the uncountable losses imposed by service activities that keep people idle, disconnected, and alienated from their own purposes in life. One way to understand leadership is to see it as waking up to people's capacities and the organizational and systemic practices that devalue and demean those capacities. Once leadership wakes us up, we face a choice. We can go back to sleep, we can leave the field, or we can join in inventing ways that bring us closer to our highest purposes.

Some of us keep track of our efforts to discover new ways to offer people with disabilities live options for active citizenship under the heading of person-centered work . The requirements for doing that work show us some of the ways that leadership is different from the exercise of authority. Working in a person-centered way can't be ordered by managers exercising command and control or advocates winning a change in law and policy. The kind of social innovation we need comes from commitments that people make to each other and to a vision of a better future in community life. There will never be only one best way to develop jobs or arrange people's homes; the point is to multiply options that provide real opportunities through collaboration with people and their allies, support workers, and other citizens and organizations. This calls for difficult learning: there are new relationships to establish; there are tough problems to define and address; there are trade-offs and sacrifices of what is not essential; there is risk; there are losses of familiar ways; there is uncertainty.*

So we need an idea of leadership that demands responsibility from everyone rather than delegating our future to people in authority or waiting for heroes to save us with guaranteed answers. Leadership is exercised through contributions that support difficult learning. Anybody can make that kind of contribution. People with disabilities and family members can provide the heat necessary to unfreeze attachments to current arrangements when they risk making their dreams for a good life known and reach across familiar boundaries to recruit new allies and resources. Person-centered planning facilitators can do their work in ways that strengthen the relationships that can contain anxiety and make conflicts productive. Support workers can dive into trying and revising new ways to assist. Professionals can risk new ways to use their knowledge. Managers can make organizational constraints clear and confined to only what is essential to organizational health. Leadership is not about expertise in treating people's impairments, though that expertise can be important. It is about struggling to free one another from the social relationships and organizational structures that hold people's lives in stasis.

What place does courage have in social innovation?

Leadership that renegotiates the boundaries of inclusion and power comes from people making commitments out of freedom. Community can't grow without people freely choosing to throw in with one another and work for what they value. Community space is diminished by clienthood, labeling and setting aside whole groups under the supervision of regulated services. Community space is in danger of being colonized by consumerism, where we act as if anything worthwhile can be bought and paid for. It takes courage to resist the strong pulls to clienthood and consumerism –where others are assigned accountability for our satisfaction and safety– and take responsibility for our freedom to

---

* To think more about this understanding of leadership read Ronald Heifetz and Marty Linsky (2002). *Leadership on the line: Staying alive through the dangers of leading.* Cambridge, ma: Harvard Business School Press.

act together. If we think about it, the very root of the word courage brings our hearts into the matter. Currently, in our concern to properly account for funds and our desire to provide what people need in the way of services, we have piled a mountain of bureaucratic requirements in the middle of relationships with people with disabilities. This demands attention to so much detail complexity that staff spend an increasing amount of time in their heads talking and writing about people. This pulls us away from live connections and abstracts us from being together in ways that let us be moved by the possibilities in each others lives.

The energy to confront the forces that devalue people flows when people listen to each other in a way that connects them at the level of their hearts. Courage is engendered whenever people come together and encourage one another to listen a bit more deeply, to act on the belief that their hard work will make a difference that matters to them, to try something that advances the edge and learn from what results.*

What astonishes me is how little support it takes for many people with disabilities to show courage by moving out into life and making good things happen. But action that shifts power and the boundaries of who "we" are can be threatening. I think this may be one reason that systems try to tame person-centered work by bureaucratizing it and enforcing set rules and procedures in the name of assuring consistency and equity. Those who want to do person-centered work within such systems have to find ways to open up spaces for relationship and commitment within the box of routine.

Those of us who have authority can defend our current organizational boundaries from the threat of greater equality with the people we serve. We won't face as much change if we drug people into stupor. We won't face as much change if we control people and obscure their own sense of purpose and interest. We won't face as much change if we police people's opportunities for new relationships and roles. But opening even a little space in highly

---

* Beth Mount and I share a process that supports direct service workers to join a person that they support in a learning journey that calls on this kind of courage in *Make a difference: A guidebook for person-centered direct support* which you can order from www.inclusion.com

controlled environments can generate enough energy for cracks to open and let new light in. People are inspiring in their ability to find resources when they have found purpose.

How has innovation in service provision affected person-centered work?

I would have thought that increasing service competence would result in a rising curve in the effectiveness of person-centered work. But that doesn't seem to be what's happening.

Take employment for people with substantial needs for assistance. As a field we used to imagine that work was impossible for them. But social innovations reaching back to the early 1970's have compounded our capacity to support people in good jobs: we know more and more about discovering people's capacities, about modifying or designing job roles that provide a good fit, about systematic instruction, about making the best of technological support, about collaborating with employers and co-workers, about minimizing benefits traps, about responding to some peoples' desire for their own businesses. This impressive progress should provide far better odds for work when people are planning their futures and open a variety of interesting contexts for person-centered support. In some places this is exactly what has happened.

But in many other places person-centered plans mount up but the numbers of people employed remains very small. In these places the growing distance between what evidence demonstrates is reasonable to expect in the way of employment and what these systems continue to provide has not set a new standard that mobilizes change. Instead, those organizations deploy a variety of defensive maneuvers, most of which are adapted from those who have held the line against offering people a real alternative to institutionalization: People aren't asking for work. People are happy not working and shouldn't be disturbed. People will lose more than they ever could gain by working. It is disrespectful, not to mention unrealistic, to suggest that people have an obligation to work. People choose not to work and we must not question their choice.

This is one more instance of the powerful and often unspoken effects of current structures on the content of plans. Thoughtful practitioners of person-centered planning will ask themselves whether the plans they assist people to make reflect what is really possible or unthinkingly defend imposing unrealistic limits on what people can achieve.

How can we minimize stereotypes and biases against people with disabilities?

Robert Putnam, the political scientist who's done so much to show the importance of social relationships to our wellbeing, has said that what our society requires for its very survival is a more expansive sense of "**we**". There is no way to move toward that bigger **we** abstractly. The way there is through building real relationships among real people who initially look to each other like "them". Stereotypes live in the world of assumption and abstraction. Practical experience of our interdependencies in pursuit of things that matter to us overcomes stereotypes, even experiences as simple as a shared meal.

The motor of person-centered work is imagining better and then taking steps together toward better. When we notice the power of stereotypes to shape responses to people with disabilities, we've identified a major lever for change. The first thing to do is wake up to the reality of stereotyping, not just as something that those bad people out there do, but as something that we're all liable to.

One sign that we're trapped is a sense (often unspoken) of certainty that we know all we need to know about a person. This is worth examining when it supports the assumption that however things are now is about as good as things can be -maybe with some small adjustments or extras. Sometimes we assert that things are as good as possible because we have other demands on our time, or we need a rest, or we can't figure out how to make room in our organization's life for something new. These reasons are only a problem if we hide them and say that the person alone is the source of the limitation and therefore refuse to own our part of the situation. If we get too deep into the belief that we've done all that's possible, we'll fall asleep and miss our chances to learn.

If we're willing wake up, we can put ourselves at a person's disposal with an attitude of openness and curiosity. This is a posture that says, before and beneath any words, "There is a lot that I don't know about you and I want to learn something more of who you are." For at least a moment, this shifts the locus of control. The person becomes guide and teacher, with whatever support might be necessary. By looking and listening with appreciative questions in mind, we can discover interests and capacities that will break us out of the stereotype trap.

When services stop reinforcing the stories that justify segregation and power-over, people with disabilities can carry out the most effective form of public education there is: meeting their fellow citizens in ordinary roles in regular places. This opens up a space for people to discover that "common sense" about people like "them" is not the real story. The real story is about people with significant differences finding satisfying ways to live, work, learn, and play together with their fellow citizens. The real story is about the struggles and rewards of creating a more expansive we.

What is discrimination?

Discrimination is the ability to see difference. When we sense difference among wines or flowers we become connoisseurs. In the context of disability, discrimination is too seldom a process of close and appreciative study of the ways a particular person's impairments influence their capacity to make an important contribution to our common life. Too often discrimination is about devaluing difference, mindlessly seeing difference as somehow creating a second class person, somebody whose interests we don't have to regard. Somebody whose story we assume we know and whose future we think we can predict based on making a diagnosis or hearing a label. This becomes self-reinforcing when it governs the way others relate to the disabled person.

One way to think about person-centered planning is as a way to appreciate the particular difference that each unique person can make in their community and then to figure out which opportunities and support will make that positive difference possible.

How does poverty affect person-centered work?

The people who founded Beyond Welfare in Ames, Iowa, point to three kinds of poverty: not enough money, not enough friends, and not enough meaning. Obviously those three poverties don't have to go together. Some people without enough money have good relationships with lots of people and things to do that are meaningful to them. But people whose lives are controlled by services are at risk of lacking all three: the material poverty, isolation, and lack of meaningful activity in the lives of too many people with disabilities occur at considerable public expense.

Robert Putnam, the political scientist whose research has explored what he calls social capital, says the well connected are far more likely to be hired, housed, healthy, and happy. Service practices that keep people from developing social relationships in which they contribute and play a valued role undermine the chances they will find their way into greater real wealth: more friends, more meaning, enough money.

An important measure of person-centered planning is its contribution to real wealth. In addition to promoting and supporting real jobs, that means encouraging people to be bold in seeking ways to engage with what has meaning for them and resourceful in connecting with other people.

What is the principle of normalization?

If we were trying to account for the positive changes in the life chances of people with disabilities over the last 50 years, we would identify multiple, interacting streams of influence. There's an organizing stream created by strong associations of parents and powerful organizing by disabled people. There's a legal stream that culminated in the US with the Education of All Handicapped Children Act, the Americans with Disabilities Act and the Supreme Court's Olmstead decision. There is a stream of technical progress in supporting people's development and ability to act. There is a stream of innovation in the ways people can be assisted to join into educational opportunities, move into their own homes, and hold real jobs.

Another stream, the one I've put a good deal of energy into, questions how we understand the social situation of people with disabilities and what positive principles might best guide our efforts as we make the best of the opportunities and energies that the other streams generate. There are several ways to approach these questions, and there is considerable debate about which perspective and principles offer the best understanding. One useful as a foundation person-centered work came into the world of services to people with disabilities in the late 60's, as the principle of normalization. The foremost thinker about this way of understanding services is Wolf Wolfensberger, who was a professor emeritus at Syracuse University until his death in February 2011.

The basic idea is straightforward: when you are responsible for arranging the life conditions of socially devalued people, use socially valued means to achieve socially valued ends. Whenever there's a choice between a more socially typical or positive way to do something and a less socially typical way to do something, learn a way to follow the path that's more positive even though it might be harder. That sounded almost trivial until we began to notice how bereft people's lives were of what ordinary people find meaningful and how people were drowning under service practices that reinforced and justified miserably low expectations and segregation. Services put people in places that neither looked nor felt anything like home. Even good services occupied people in ways that wasted their lives.

As we developed better ways to see how people were living, we began to see more clearly how many ways we were, despite our good intentions, spending a growing public investment in services on ways of doing things that only reproduced people's exclusion and powerlessness. Because we have habits of reproducing the marginalization of people with disabilities without being mindful of doing it, we want to become more conscious of the ways that we create social distance and control and we want to work in a positive way to overcome those ways of dealing with people.

Because of the word itself, some people got the idea of creating settings and services that looked and felt normal mixed up with making people normal, as if there were something the matter with being a person with impairments and our project was to make you normal. This misunderstanding led to several efforts to refine the ideas.

The most extensive theoretical developments came from Wolfensberger himself. He concluded the capstone of effective support is that people are supported in a way that both improves their competence and improves their social interpretation such that they take up valued social roles. It's Wolfensberger's conviction that the good things in life come to those who inhabit valued social roles, so the acronym for his step beyond normalization is SRV, social role valorization.*

How did the principle of normalization influence the development of person-centered planning?
Way back in the mid-1970's, those of us who were beginning to do person-centered planning were very much involved in teaching normalization. The most powerful way that we did that was to create opportunities for learners to see a small sample of what everyday life is like for people with disabilities in a particular setting with the lenses provided by the principle of normalization. We kept discovering a fundamental mismatch between our account of what's really most important for the people we were meeting and what was actually going on in their everyday life.

These were not exotic things, just everyday things that most of us take for granted. We might say that people need a secure home that feels like their own and a service provider would agree that providing people a secure home of their own was their mission. But even a short look at the place from the point of view of normalization turned up all sorts of ways that home life was dominated by people's clienthood and congregation with other people with disabilities. Home for them looked nothing like home for me. You had to buy into a negative disability story in order to make sense of the differences you saw. These disability stories fell into pretty clear patterns. People lack private bedrooms and have roommates that they didn't choose because they live as objects of government charity and couldn't afford to be choosy. The details of people's daily lives are controlled by staff because people can't

---

*To download a summary of SRV, visit www.srvip.org/overview_SRV_Osburn.pdf for additional resources go to www.socialrolevalorization.com/resources/

learn to exercise greater self-direction because they have 2 year old minds in grown up bodies. People's movements are restricted because they are dangerous or "low functioning" and so endangered. People have no relationships outside their client group because they prefer to be with their own kind.

When we had opportunities to address these disconnects, we designed people's supports starting with the best answers we could find to a two-part question about each particular person, "Who is this person and what is most important in her life?" Then we went on to ask, "What will matter the most to her in the way that we spend public money on her behalf, in the way we structure space with her, in the way we spend time with her, in the ways we communicate with and about her, in the groupings of people that she finds herself in, and in the roles available to her."

So a number of us who originated approaches to person-centered planning were motivated by immersion in the ways in which de-institutionalization had recreated the institution in a more acceptable form, often in a less violent form, but in a form that left the social structures that exclude people pretty much intact. Person-centered planning began as one way to resist segregation and control by directly informing the way services developed.

I wish I could say that this was all in the past, but I see our field continuing to reproduce exclusion and control, and not just for the people who remain in institutions and group homes. Sadly, most person-centered planning has relatively little effect on the design of a person's services because it has been swallowed up inside existing services and planners take current settings, groupings, and routines for granted as they are. Not even the justifying disability stories have changed very much.

How do you judge the effectiveness of person-centered work?

My framework for assessing person-centered work comes from the effort a number of us made to communicate the positive implications of the principle of normalization for service design and practice. We focused on identifying the experiences that most people would value having more of in their lives and the capacities a service needs in order to skillfully support those experiences. This perspective is summarized on the following pages.

All citizens have better life chances, and everyone's world grows more interesting, when communities offer rich opportunities for all people to have these **five valued experiences:**

Belonging in a diverse variety of relationships and memberships.

Being respected as whole persons whose history, capacities and future are worthy of attention and whose gifts engage them in valued social roles.

Sharing ordinary places and activities with other citizens, neighbors, classmates, and co-workers. Living, working, learning, and playing confidently in ordinary community settings.

Contributing by discovering, developing, and giving their gifts and investing their capacities and energy in pursuits that make a positive difference to other people. There are gifts of being and gifts of doing: contributions can include interested presence as well as capable performance. Contributions may be freely exchanged or earn pay.

Choosing what they want in everyday situations in ways that reflect their highest purpose. Having the freedom, support, information, and assistance to make the same choices as others of a similar age and learning to make wiser choices over time. Being encouraged to use and strengthen voice regardless of mode of communication, clarify what really matters, make thoughtful decisions, and learn from experience.

The quest to act in ways that offer more of these five interrelated experiences builds a more competent community. Healthy communities work to notice and overcome *us and them* thinking by exercising social creativity in doing these **five community tasks.**

Promoting interdependence by valuing and investing in the social ties and associations that promote trust , encourage mutual support, and energize collaboration.

Living inclusive stories by opening valued social roles to people who have been excluded by prejudice, stereotyped expectations, and poorly designed opportunities and by celebrating the benefits of diversity.

Practicing hospitality by making ordinary places acceptable and welcoming and finding effective ways to adapt to and accommodate differences that might otherwise keep people out.

Seeing and supporting capacities by adopting the practice of using what the community has to get more of what it really needs, looking first at community assets and what people can contribute rather than getting stuck on what is missing or scarce.

Resolving conflicts in fair and creative ways. When people whose voices have been missing begin to speak up about their interests and concerns, new problems come up about who has power and how it will be used. Healthy communities avoid escaping into withdrawal, exclusion or violence and find ways to work together and find ways that more people can stay involved and get more of what really matters to them.

History shows that people with disabilities are vulnerable to isolation, wasted capacities, and excessive external control. Common practices in the world of services too often force people to live in a box that limits their opportunities for valued experiences in order to get the assistance that they need.

> **Segregation** at the margins of community life, which decreases the chances of building a more diverse community.
>
> **Stereotypes** that stick people into a narrow range of social roles that reinforce stories of incompetence, unworthiness, unacceptability, and passivity.
>
> **Congregation**: involuntarily grouping people together in special, separate groups based on their professionally applied label.
>
> **Poor support** because of unrealistically low expectations, technical incompetence, or lack of imagination and creativity.
>
> **External control** that deprives people of choices because of a low level of individualization or a reflex response to vulnerability.

Service workers who want to assist people with disabilities to get or keep out of the box have to build alliances that are strong enough and plans that are imaginative enough to energize creative action that opens pathways for people's energy, capacities, and gifts to flow into community life. They continue to improve the quality of their answers to the questions that define **five accomplishments**.

> **How can we assist people to make and sustain connections, memberships and friendships?** Service workers make a difference when they listen deeply and act thoughtfully to provide exactly what a person needs to build a bridge to community participation.
>
> **How do we enhance people's reputation?** Respect comes to those who play recognizable and valued parts in everyday life. Service workers make a difference when they support people to identify and take up social roles that express their interests and provide needed assistance with negotiating the accommodations they need to be successful and so encourage valued social roles.
>
> **How do we increase people's active involvement in the life of our communities?** Service workers make a difference when they assist people to make the most of the ordinary community settings that attract their interest and energy. This increases community presence.
>
> **How do we assist people to develop and invest their gifts and capacities?** Service workers make a difference when they focus on what each person can bring to others and bring imagination and technical competence to designing and delivering the help each person needs to develop competency.
>
> **How do we increase choice and control in people's lives?** Service workers make a difference when they honor people's rights and responsibilities and offer what works to promote their autonomy.

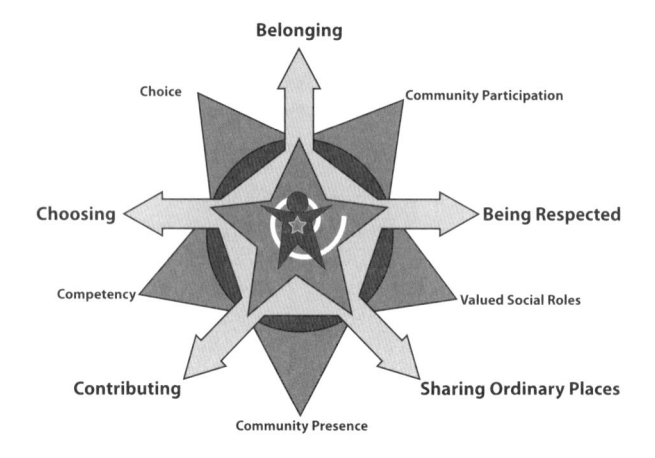

Diagram with arrows radiating outward labeled: Belonging, Community Participation, Being Respected, Valued Social Roles, Sharing Ordinary Places, Community Presence, Contributing, Competency, Choosing, Choice.

When person-centered work is effective at the personal level, everyday experience changes for the person and other community members. The places where a person is actively engaged shift from human service settings to a growing range of ordinary community places including workplaces and ordinary homes. The person spends more time enjoying the respect that comes with filling valued social roles. The person's competencies increase; they have a growing capacity to act from their gifts. The person has a greater range of choices and a greater sense of self-efficacy in choosing and working toward goals that matter to them. Most important, the person belongs and experiences a variety of good relationships that includes both disabled people and people without identified disabilities. These new experiences challenge and change whatever everyday community and workplace practices that keep people with disabilities at a distance.

When person-centered work influences an organization's innovation agenda, the organizations capacities to support these experiences and engage community challenges expand.

What is the purpose of person-centered work?

Person-centered work serves different purposes in different contexts.

As more systems require person-centered plans, I think the most common and least interesting purpose is to perform a required procedure that often includes some conversation about a person's wishes and then to fill in and file a form labeled "person-centered plan". In this context, the question that person-centered planning is trying to answer is, "How do we follow the rules?" There is very little uncertainty to cope with in this context.

More interesting things happen when a service organization commits itself to make changes within its current structure and culture to improve the fit between what staff offer and a person's needs, preferences and interests. The organization that looks for better ways to do what's important to people as well as what's important for them, for example. In that context the people who receive service get real benefits; staff go beyond holding meetings and follow a path to working in a person-centered way. In this context, the question that person-centered work is trying to answer is, "How do we use what we already have to better meet this person's needs and accommodate his preferences?" There is some uncertainty to cope with in this context.

A third context for person-centered work happens outside the typical boundaries and culture of many current service organizations. This context emerges when people with disabilities and their allies join in intentional efforts to shift the social position of people with disabilities by strengthening the direct and visible contribution a person makes to community life. This involves working out the innovations necessary for a person to participate more fully, give more, and get more from communities they share with people who are not disabled. The question is, "How can we invent what's necessary for this person to show up in ordinary community life as a valued friend and a contributing citizen?" There can be a lot of uncertainty to cope with in this context; that's why its important to convene a person's allies and give them the opportunity to commit themselves to supporting the person's efforts.

How do you see the difference between person-centered work and typical service practice?

From its founding our field followed a pattern of matching the individual problems that professionals defined with solutions from the professional repertoire: determine what the matter with the person is, select the best treatment solution for that condition, and then apply the solution, modifying it as necessary. That pattern of thought and action works to organize responses to lots of well defined human situations for which we have adequate technical responses –non-experimental brain surgery and docking a space shuttle for example. It doesn't work particularly well for people with substantial and enduring impairments. This is because we lack the technology to solve the problem so completely that assistance is no longer necessary. And it is because substantial impairments can become life-defining when they cast the person into the role of 24 hour client for life. Professional inability to repair what professionals define as broken too often relegates these embarrassments to professional competence not just to the edges of society but even to the edges of our services. Back wards hid the people institutions had no tools to fix. Today we hide people in nursing homes behind stories about "medical fragility" and in the back rooms of day programs behind stories of "challenging behavior ".

Person-centered work is based on a different understanding of impairments. We have come to a better understanding of this perspective as disabled people have raised their voices to criticize the dehumanization implied in seeing whole people as problems to be remedied (or prevented considering the current rate of pregnancy terminations when disability is detected). On this view, impairments are dimensions of human diversity–sometimes complex and troubling dimensions, but integral aspects of a whole person. Having a bundle of neurophysiological differences that can be labeled "autism" makes up an important part of the way this particular persons person is in the world. Living out a different way of being in consequence of these differences is one more way to be human and only compromises people's equality as human beings if the difference is mis-recognized as justification for segregation and control instead of understood as an invitation to accommodation and well tailored assistance.

There is no doubt that some differences call for mindfulness and creativity in joining the person to deal with those differences that get in the person's way and discovering the exact settings and roles in which the person can discover, develop and give their gifts. Person-centered work is about assisting people to discover what they have to give, recruit the people that can make it possible for them to give it, and learn what mixture of technology, accommodations, learning and assistance have the best chance to make their contributions possible. A big part of this work is encouraging people to mobilize the alliances that they need to push back against the force that wants to box them into a setting that separates and supervises them.

Are there people for whom person-centered planning doesn't work?

Let's be sure we distinguish between planning meetings, which are optional, and working in a person-centered way, which is what all of us who offer assistance owe the people who rely on us no matter how frustrating, disappointing, and difficult the relationship might be from time to time for all concerned.

As for meeting to make plans. Some people know what they want and have what they need to get it. Making them go through a complex planning process is a waste of their time.

Some people's lives are controlled by organizations with very little will to shape what they offer to respond to a person's particular life journey. Very few people with disabilities will challenge the staff they count on beyond the first non-verbal signs of staff anxiety or irritation about requests for change. So people with disabilities will mostly be docile and plans will mostly call for more of the same, perhaps recording a slightly more ambitious holiday wish or a request for a different activity off the existing menu. In these circumstances not much of importance to the person will be discussed in any depth and not much will happen.

When people with disabilities don't have allies –people that they know are on their side, believing in them, and willing to offer active support – the process will be paced by the rate at which others are willing to make offers to accompany the person in a new way. When the planning circle is filled with staff and perhaps family members who are too busy to add anything to their current commitments, the process will tend to be shallow and lack traction in the world outside the meeting until shared experience builds up stronger alliances.

Probably the most painful situations are in meeting people who lack even the memory of a secure attachment to someone who cares for them without reserve. Urie Bronfenbrenner, the Cornell developmental psychology professor, was once asked in a media interview what the necessary condition of human development was. He had a clear answer: No human being develops fully unless there is or has been at least one other person who is irrationally attached to them; unless there's at least one other person who's crazy in love with them.

Now one of the ways that some people with disabilities were wounded in their growing up is that they missed this attachment, often through being institutionalized as infants or children or being in a family or a series of foster families without the emotional resources to care for them. This lack of attachment can show up in all sorts of relationship and self-regulation difficulties: trouble with trust, self-control, emotion, thinking, imagining.

Sometimes the understanding of a person's history that can emerge from person-centered planning can open the heart of someone in the planning circle and encourage them into the rigors of a closer more enduring relationship with the person who lives with this interior isolation. Though the effects of being thrown on your own in early life often last a lifetime, people can find relationships in which beautiful things begin to happen alongside the wounds.

A person's isolation and its consequences may suggest that it's a good idea to invest considerable time in building up stronger relationships by sharing life experiences with a person before calling a planning meeting, It may make sense to offer the person the experience of having their history heard by people who are willing to listen deeply to what has hurt and what has built the person's capacities rather than jumping straight into dreams and goals. But there is no reason to shy away from person-centered planning based on a person's difficult life circumstances.

What conditions increase the effectiveness of person-centered work?

Resisting the forces of social devaluation requires all the people involved to act from their freedom. If people can't say no, then yes doesn't mean very much. But many human service settings are zones of compliance in which relationships are subordinated to and constrained by complex and detailed rules. In those environments, unless staff commit themselves to be people's allies and treat the rules and boundaries and structures as constraints to be creatively engaged as opposed to simply conforming, person-centered work will be limited to improving the conditions of people's confinement in services.

Commitment freely given is one necessary condition. Another is thoughtful organizational investment in innovation. The kind of innovation I mean starts from deep listening to a person -their words, their bodies as they are situated in the settings they encounter, and the images, connections and storylines that have power and meaning for them. This kind of listening underwrites agreements to search for opportunities and figure out what will assist the person to make the best of them. This generates a learning cycle of trying things and building on what works. Individual learning cycles shape demands for innovation at the organizational and system level.

Innovation depends on an organization's capacity to manage multiple, conflicting constraints in a responsible and resourceful way. Money is limited (often because it is sunk in structures that accept rather than challenge the idea that people with disabilities belong in groups with "their own kind" under staff control). Requirements for compliance are real. What an innovating organization does is give the demand for change that arises from listening to people a strong enough voice to influence the ways an organization manages money, structure, boundaries and rules.

There are four massively underutilized resources in most organizations. The passion and capacities of people with disabilities, the concern and assets of families, the talents and connections of direct support workers, and the assets in communities outside the borders of human services. A culture of control keeps organizations from appreciating these possibilities for power-with and locks people into power-over relationships. Attention goes one-sidedly to deficiencies, to negative assessments of motives, to the potential for rejection, failure, neglect and abuse. Organizations that mobilize the resources hidden by a relentlessly negative scan invest in an appreciative search to reveal and connect people's higher purposes and capacities and commit themselves to driving out fear and distrust by investing in opportunities for people to listen carefully to one another, search for new possibilities, and struggle with one another to make and follow through on a series of more and more interesting agreements about what they are willing to work for together.

Person centered planning is a forum in which concerned people can talk, listen, think about what they next want to create together. It's a place to review what they have learned, name conflicts, notice opportunities for creative action agree on some steps forward. As I understand it, this forum is a place of power-with, not power-over.

People with disabilities have experienced other sorts of planning meetings as power-over settings in which staff dictate. To correct this, some people have changed the label to person-directed planning and designed a forum in which the person with a disability is in charge, deciding on the agenda, the process, and the results. I can't help noticing that this risks becoming a forum for power-over by just flipping over who directs and who is directed in the meeting. One downside of this is that many people with developmental disabilities who count on assistance have very little actual control of their daily situations, so the capacity to deliver what the person decides may be very limited. Following a person's lead is very different from putting her in charge of a planning process. Of course we collaborate with people before their planning meeting to figure out what will make it easiest for them to be heard and join in the thinking, but we want to create conditions in which the person is able to listen and explore as well as to speak and direct a meeting. The social creativity necessary to support a good life in community more often results from effective interdependency than a single will. Real change is a matter of power-with and happens when people become allies for a shared purpose.

Alliances are more likely to happen when people cultivate the qualities of a group that gets things done: the choice to listen deeply; the ability to see capacity and seek possibility and learning; commitment to believe in each other and to honor agreements; and the willingness to be moved by another person's purposes and projects. The importance of alliances makes person-centered work fundamentally a process of convening people and giving them the chance to strengthen their sense of common purpose and commitment to one another.

Build Alliances

Beth Mount

Index

A
Approaches to person-centered planning
   Cultivating True Livelihood 63, 69
   Essential Lifestyle Planning 45
   Framework for Planning 107
   MAPS 80
   PATH 81
   Personal Futures Planning 27
   Person-centered Thinking Tools 47, 51

C
Capacity view 19, 25, 34, 35, 57, 76, 94
Citizenship 19, 23, 59, 88, 110
Community 11, 24, 29, 62, 84, 92, 100
   Asset Based Community Development 87
   Connecting 29, 62, 66, 96, 118
Consumerism 11, 105
Courage 26, 43, 71, 115

E
Employment 62, 101, 117
   Person-centered job development 63, 103
Evaluating person-centered planning 28, 55, 79, 123
Exclusion 9, 23, 60, 99, 111

H
History of person-centered work 27, 45, 48, 76, 107, 122

I
Implementation 43
Inspiration 24, 45, 61, 75, 88

L

Leadership 21, 26, 41, 60, 100, 114

Limits of person-centered planning 21, 47, 53, 84, 106, 129

M

Meaning of person-centered work 26, 57, 61, 73, 76, 89, 105, 127

O

Organizational change 21, 39, 47, 49, 54, 130
    Appreciative Inquiry 4D Cycle 37

R

Rights 63, 89, 110

U

Understanding of Disability 11, 23, 109

Learning More

This is the third in a series of books about person-centered work from Inclusion Press. Their contents are included here to make it easier to find more to read about topics raised in these interviews and to identify additional writers with important things to say about person-centered work.

Order from www.inclusion.com.

Implementing Person-Centered Planning
Voices of Experience

A Turn for the Better

> Pete Ritchie identifies the defining features of person-centered planning, provides an example of planning with a person who uses mental health services, and describes better and worse ways to implement person-centered planning.

The Origins of Person-Centered Planning

> Connie Lyle O'Brien and John O'Brien write a history of the emergence of person-centered planning in terms of communities of practice.

A Plan Is Not an Outcome

> Michael Smull advocates changing the service system by combining person-centered planning with control of available resources so that people can move toward living the life they want.

Community-Building & Commitment-Building

> David and Faye Wetherow describe the process of helping people rethink their ways of understanding as they make plans with individuals, groups, and communities.

Increasing the Chances for Deep Change

> Beth Mount, John O'Brien and Connie Lyle O'Brien identify twelve resources that each increase the chances that person-centered planning will make a significant difference in people's lives.

The Value of Measuring Person-Centered Planning
> Steve Holburn argues for the importance of systematically measuring the fidelity with which person-centered planning is implemented and the ways people's lives change as a result and provides an annotated bibliography on measuring the processes and outcome

Opening the Door
> David Pitonyak explodes typical ways of understanding challenging behavior by describing what he has learned in his relationship with Danny about what really matters in person-centered work.

Two Is Not Enough
> Mary Romer identifies lessons from her family experience that energize and direct her work in person-centered planning.

The Weird Guy
> Steve Holburn shows another facet of his talent in a short story about encountering capacity.

Great Questions and The Art of Portraiture
> John O'Brien defines the basic question in person-centered planning and connects facilitation with the work of sociologist Sara Lawrence-Lightfoot.

The Art and Soul of Person-Centered Planning
> Beth Mount explores artistic creation as integral to the process of person-centered planning.

The Rhode Island Facilitators Forum
> Jo Krippenstapel reflects on the experience of increasing the numbers and the capacities of people able to facilitate planning.

Some Words Along the Way
> Mary Jo Alimena Caruso and Kathy Lee gather the reflections of participants in a long term project to develop competent facilitators.

Helping Staff Support Choice
> Michael Smull provides a helpful way to clarify staff responsibility in situations that can become confused as people's freedom increases.

Communication Ally
> Meyer Shevin shows how well-meaning people can deny people with communication impairments the opportunity to participate in their own planning and defines a key role that provides a missing link in person-centered planning.

Getting Beyond Sick
> Karen Green McGowan defines medical obstacles to development for people with profound disabilities and shows the health benefits of different ways of thinking and planning.

Mutual Learning
> Susannah Joyce, Betty Boomer, and John Jones describe fine-tuning the person-centered planning process in collaboration with people who use mental health services.

Sequoia
> Sally Sehmsdorf demonstrates the process of creating an invitation to person-centered planning for senior parents and their families.

Pathfinders
> Connie Lyle O'Brien, Beth Mount, John O'Brien and Fredda Rosen describe a person-centered development process that supports some young people and their families to escape from segregated services and participate as adults in the opportunities offered by living in New York City.

Large Group Process for Person-Centered Planning
> Connie Lyle O'Brien and John O'Brien identify the benefits of large group processes for person-centered planning Marsha Threlkeld joins in to describe how the process traveled to the Seattle area.

A Simple Half-Hitch
> Debra McLean outlines her method of using person-centered planning in assisting people to succeed at jobs that match their interests and talents.

Vocational Profiles
> Anne O'Bryan discusses the use of vocational profiles –a form of person-centered planning focused on supported employment– in the process of discovering good jobs.

Some Beginnings
> Jach Pealer & Sandy Landis describe a process for influencing a state's plans for deinstitutionalization and a way to assist people to create personal histories. They also reflect on how change happens.

Thinking About Support Broker Roles
> Michael Smull defines the systemic and organizational conditions necessary for the success of service coordination and presents the person-centered plan as a framework for learning.

Person-Centered Teams
> Helen Sanderson outlines and illustrates a team development process aimed at assuring that person-centered plans are implemented in the daily reality of service settings.

The Challenges of Person-Centered Work
> Patrica Fratangelo and Jeff Strully identify the personal and organizational transformations that moved their two agencies from group-based programs to personalized supports.

Planning with People
> Martin Routledge, Helen Sanderson and Rob Greig describe the development of guidance on person-centered planning from the English Department of Health, summarize its key points, and outline their efforts to support local implementation.

A Little Book About Person-Centered Planning

The Power in Vulnerability

> Judith Snow places person-centered planning in the context of interdependence and community.
>
> *When I am in relationship with other individuals and if these others are networked with each other and especially if these others are different from each other, the possibility exists for all of us to have a rich life, drawing on each other's gifts. Differences in each other's physical and cognitive functioning, our interests, history and experience, our possibilities, our possessions and resources only add to the mix of possibilities that increase our total capacity.*

Learning to Listen

> John O'Brien and Connie Lyle O'Brien reflect on listening, the foundation skill for person-centered planning.
>
> *People come to life when they make contact with someone who works actively and faithfully to understand what they want to say. When people communicate in unusual ways, or when they have been rendered invisible by an environment that discounts the worth of their communication, the effects of listening can be profoundly energizing.*

Person-Centered Planning Has Arrived… or Has it?

> Connie Lyle O'Brien, John O'Brien, and Beth Mount identify issues that arise as service systems mandate person-centered planning.
>
> *We believe that implementations of person-centered planning will be disappointing if people rigorously apply a procedure without sufficient regard for the context of relationships and agreements necessary for it to thrive.*

Think Before You Plan

> Michael Smull defines issues for facilitators to consider before agreeing to plan.
>
> *Be sure to think before you plan. Thinking about a few issues before you get started can help you achieve a better outcome, prevent problems, avoid unnecessary struggle, and save you from public embar-*

rassment. {Plans are} ordinary, day to day efforts to understand how someone wants to live and what we are going to do about it. The overriding principle is that a plan is not an outcome, the life that the person wants is the outcome. The only acceptable reason to plan is to help someone move toward the life they desire.

The Politics of Person-Centered Planning

John O'Brien and Connie Lyle O'Brien situate person-centered planning in terms of enduring conflicts that arise at the intersection of individual and family life, community, and human service policy and practice.

Person-centered planning belongs to the politics of community and disability. It is not a way to avoid conflict; it is one way to seek real and enduring conflicts in collaboration with people with disabilities who want to consider a change in their lives.

Revisiting Choice

Michael Smull identifies common abuses and misunderstandings of "choice" in the lives of people with disabilities and provides guidance on dealing with situations when it seems impossible to honor a person's choice, finding balance between choice and safety, creating the kind of opportunities that increase capacity to honor people's preferences about how they want to live, and increasing people's control over their lives.

What opportunities we provide, hold back, encourage people to find or protect people from depends as much on our values as they do on the preferences and capacities of the people we support. We need to listen to ourselves when we say that someone is not ready or that they should be able to do something simply because it is their choice. Our values influence and often control what we support. We need to talk about what our values are so that we understand the basis on which we are making decisions. We need to remember that the opportunities that are made available depend on the values of those with control.

Positive Ritual and Quality of Life
> Michael Smull raises consciousness about the routines and rituals that structure our days and embody our relationships.

As we look at supporting people in their communities we need to remember that much of the richness of community comes from the relationships that we have and the rituals that celebrate and build those relationships… In our rapidly changing, mobile, and fragmented society, positive rituals deserve attention for all of us regardless of the presence of disability. For people who need substantial support to get through life, developing positive rituals should be a priority.

More Than a Meeting
> Beth Mount identifies the benefits and limitations of person-centered planning, identifies ten conditions associated with positive changes in people's lives and outlines the framework for person-centered development projects.

People interested in the future of person-centered planning must look past the lure of the quick fix toward the long journey of learning to do things differently on personal, community, and organizational levels. The resources of the system can be used to support safe havens where people can learn the art of person-centered development. The continuing challenge is to create environments which nurture the concern, commitment, and caring that engenders true relationships.

The Quest for Community Membership
> John O'Brien and Connie Lyle O'Brien use the image of a quest to explore the relationship between person-centered planning and community building.

How can person-centered planning contribute to building communities competent to include people with developmental disabilities as contributing members? Failure to actively and thoughtfully engage this tough question unnecessarily limits the effectiveness of the growing variety of approaches to person-centered planning.

After the Plan

Michael Smull outlines a learning process for closing the gap between how people want to live and how their services are supporting them to live.

Whenever people are empowered a dynamic situation is created. The process of listening and then acting on what has been heard is an ongoing cycle. What people want today will be different from what they want tomorrow. The process is lifelong and interactive. The only thing worse than never listening is only listening once.

Participation Through Support Circles

Judith Snow moves outside the confines of a disability focus to describe the steps to circle building.

Circles empower circle members because they are unpredictable. Energized by multiple, complex relationships they often become magnets of synergy, taking advantage of lucky accidents –opportunities that cannot be predicted or bureaucratically managed into existence. This living essence of circles drives out the deadening spirit of disability thinking.

A Circle Check-Up

John O'Brien and Jeff Strully offer a list of questions that support circle members can use to assess their contribution to supporting people.

Circle members hold responsibility for developing a deep, accurate and clear account of the person's interests, preferences and dreams and assuring that this understanding guides the day-to-day behavior of the people who provide assistance.

The Ethics of MAPS and PATH

Jack Pearpoint and Marsha Forest define dangers and safeguards in the use of person-centered planning and provide a checklist for good facilitation.

Good facilitators hold questions with people, then wait, and listen to the silence. The tension in this silence creates a safe space for people to fill with their deep yearnings and simple unspoken needs, the real stuff of life. As facilitators we open an inviting space for the focus person and insure that their ideas and wishes are heard. Then the hard work begins.

Telling New Stories

> John O'Brien and Beth Mount differentiate person-centered planning from planning that serves systems by contrasting two different sorts of stories about people's lives and the role of service providers with them.
>
> *Burton Blatt said, "Some stories enhance life; others degrade it. So we must be careful about the stories we tell, about the ways that we define ourselves and other people."*

Finding a Way Toward Everyday Lives: The Contribution of Person-centered Planning.

> John O'Brien and Herb Lovett identify what different approaches to person-centered planning have in common, discuss the ways person-centered planning influences change, consider its limitations, and define some of the controversies among practitioners.
>
> *Person-centered planning can invite, align, and direct shared efforts to create positive community roles for people with disabilities. It allows people to exercise their practical wisdom to work for more inclusive, more just communities… The future of person-centered planning depends on the willingness and ability of its practitioners to improve through critical reflection on the effects of their work in the lives of people with disabilities and their families.*

A Guide to Personal Futures Planning

> John O'Brien considers the role planning plays in improving the lives of people with substantial disabilities, defines five essential accomplishments of human services as a perspective on service quality, and outlines a very early version of the procedure for personal futures planning.
>
> *None of us creates our lives alone. We each create better quality life experiences with the other people who form our social network. And usually we are resources to each other without much formal planning. Like all of us, people with severe disabilities develop in relationship. But because they rely on other people's cooperation to an unusual extent, and because human services often play a larger than ordinary role in their lives, people with severe disabilities count on other's planning and organizing skills.*

INCLUSION PRESS ORDER FORM

47 Indian Trail, Toronto, ON Canada M6R 1Z8
Tel: 416-658-5363 Fax: 416-658-5067
e: inclusionpress@inclusion.com
WEB: www.inclusion.com

Inclusion SPECIAL PACKS

The Community PACK - Members of Each Other & Celebrating the Ordinary - 2 books - J O'Brien & C O'Brien
The Education Book PACK - Inclusion: Recent Research & Inclusion: How To - 2 Books - Gary Bunch
Inclusion Classics Book PACK [Action for Inclusion + Inclusion Papers]
Inclusion Classics DVD PACK (DVD or video) - [With a Little Help from My Friends + Kids Belong Together]
PATH in ACTION PACK (DVD format, video also available)
 - 2 PATH Training "Videos" (DVD) [PATH in Action + PATH Training + the PATH Workbook]
Petroglyphs PACK - Book & Video on Inclusion in High Schools - from UNH
PlayFair Teams Kit - (Teacher's book, Advocate's book , Intro CD, 2 posters)
When Spider Webs Unite PACK - Shafik Asante - Book and DVD/Video
Golden Reflections PACK - Mike Yale - Book and audio MP3

BOOKS

ABCD:When People Care Enough to Act - ABCD in Action - Mike.Green
Action for Inclusion - Classic on Inclusion
All My Life's a Circle Expanded Edition- Circles, MAPS & PATH
The All Star Company - Team Building by Nick Marsh
Atlas of Literacy & Disability
The BIG Plan - A Good Life After School - EXPANDED V2 Coulson & Simmons
Celebrating the Ordinary   John O'Brien, Connie Lyle O'Brien & Gail Jacob
Circle of Friends by Bob & Martha Perske
Circles of Adults - Colin Newton & Derek Wilson (UK)
Community Lost & Found Arthur Lockhart & Michael Clarke
The Community Place: Kate Foran with B. Jackson, P. Beeman, G. Ducharme   Ebook Version: $15.00
Conversations on Citizenship & Person-Centered Planning - New - O'Brien & Blessing - **NEW**
Creating Circles of Friends - Colin Newton & Derek Wilson (UK)
Directory of Disability Organizations in Canada (2007-08 edition)
Do You Hear What I Hear? - Janice Fialka & Karen Mikus
Dream Catchers & Dolphins Marsha Forest and Jack Pearpoint
Each Belongs - Jim Hansen with Leyden, Bunch, Pearpoint (book with CD)
Equity, Social Justice and Disability in Schools - Gary Bunch et al - **NEW**
Finding Meaning in the Work - (CD + Manual/Curriculum) (O'Briens)
Free to Fly - A Story of Manic Depression   Caroline Fei-Yeng Kwok
Friends & Inclusion: Five Approaches to Building Relationships: P. Hutchison; J. Lord, K. Lord (NEW)
From Behind the Piano - by Jack Pearpoint & **What's Really Worth Doing** by Judith Snow
     - **Now in ONE Book** (printed together)   (also see new book - Who's Drawing the Lines? - J. Snow)
Golden Reflections   - Mike Yale (also available as an MP3 - also $25)
Hints for Graphic Facilitators   - Jack Pearpoint
The Inclusion Papers - Strategies & Stories - Forest & Pearpoint editors
Inclusion: How To   Essential Classroom Strategies - Gary Bunch
Inclusion: Recent Research   G. Bunch & A. Valeo
Incurably Human   Micheline Mason
It Matters - Lessons from my Son - Janice Fialka
Kids, Disabilities Regular Classrooms   Gary Bunch
Lessons for Inclusion Curriculum Ideas for Inclusion in Elementary Schools
A Little Book About Person Centered Planning
     John O'Brien & Connie Lyle O'Brien with Forest, Lovett, Mount, Pearpoint, Small, Snow, and Strully
Make a Difference: Direct Support Guidebook (J. O'Brien & B. Mount)

PATH & MAPS Handbook: Person-Centered Ways to Build Community (NEW)
Supporting Learners with Intellectual Challenge Gary Bunch
Voices of Experience: Implementing Person-Centered Planning   Eds: John O'Brien & Connie Lyle O'Brien
Waddie Welcome & the Beloved Community   Tom Kohler & Susan Earl
When Spider Webs Unite Community & Inclusion - Shafik Asante
Who's Drawing the Lines? - Judith Snow - new autobiography - 1st of three
Yes! She Knows She's Here Nicola Schaefer's Book about Kathrine
Inclusion – Exclusion Poster (18 X 24)
Person Centered Direct Support Foldout (call for bulk rates)

MEDIA: DVDs • CD-ROMs • Videos

ABCD in ACTION - DVD-Mike Green, Henry Moore & John McKnight
Dream Catchers - Dreams & Circles - VHS video only
Doing Our Best Work: 10 Ingredients of Qualilty Support - Peter Leidy - DVD
EVERYONE Has a GIFT   J McKnight - Building Communities of Capacity - (DVD or VHS Video)
Facilitation for Inclusion with PATH & MAPS - New training DVD - Kahn & Pearpoint - **NEW**
Finding Meaning in the Work - (CD + Manual/Curriculum) - John O'Brien & Connie Lyle O'Brien
Friendship DVD/Video   Judith Snow, Marsha Forest & Jack Pearpoint on Friendship (VHS $25)
Gentle Heart Fearless Mind: Mindfulness DVD + Booklet: Alan Sloan - **NEW**
The Inclusion Classics - DVD (2 classic inclusion videos on DVD or Video)
Kids Belong Together - MAPS & Circles (DVD or VHS Video) (VHS $25)
Make a Difference: Leader's Resource Kit (Instructor's book + CD)
The MAPS Collection - DVD (2 MAPS Training videos on DVD)
Miller's MAP - MAPS in Action   (DVD or VHS Video)   (VHS $25)
My Life, My Choice - DVD   (7 stories of adults with full lives)
New MAPS TRAINING DVD   (Shafik//MAPS Process/Judith on Dreaming) (DVD or VHS Video)
The PATH Collection - DVD (2 PATH Training videos on DVD)
PATH Demo Video   Univ of Dayton Ohio - Video of Workshop on PATH
PATH in ACTION   Working with Groups -Training DVD/Video for Path with Groups
PATH TRAINING DVD   Intro Training DVD/Video - An Individual Path {Joe's Path}   (VHS $25)
Person Centered Direct Support - CD - 4 minute video & powerpoint
PlayFair Teams CD-ROM   An introduction to PlayFair Teams
ReDiscovering MAPS Charting Your Journey - MAPS training (DVD or VHS Video)
TOOLS for CHANGE - The CD-Rom for Person Centred Planning
When Spider Webs Unite - DVD/Video   and book - Shafik Asante in Action
With a Little Help from My Friends + Kids Belong Together   Circles & MAPS - (DVD or VHS Video)

July, 2011 Listing

- **Facilitation for Inclusion with PATH & MAPS** - New training **DVD**
- **Conversations on Citizenship & Person-Centered Planning** - New
- **Who's Drawing the Lines? -** Judith Snow - new
- **Equity, Social Justice and Disability in Schools -** Gary Bunch et al - new
- **PATH & MAPS Handbook:** Person-Centered Ways to Build Community (NEW)
- **Gentle Heart Fearless Mind:** Mindfulness DVD + Booklet: Alan Sloan (NEW)
- **Friends & Inclusion:** Five Approaches to Building Relationships: P. Hutchison; J. Lord, K. Lord (NEW)
- **Golden Reflections:** by Vargus (Mike's seeing-eye guide dog) with Mike Yale Also in Audio MP3
- **Planning for a Real Life After School:** Transition from School (2 editions)
- **The Poetry of David Moreau:**   If You're Happy and You Know It Clap Your Hand
- **Doing Our Best Work:** 10 Ingredients of Quality Support: Peter Leidy - DVD
- **ABCD in Action** - DVD & Book -When People Care Enough to Act
- **My Life My Choice** - DVD - Seven Adults living full lives in the community
- **Make a Difference** - book; Leaders Guide, Work Booklets
- **The Big Plan** - A Good Life After School - Transition Planning with groups
- **Each Belongs** - book & CD - The 1st Inclusive School Board ever!
- **PlayFair Teams** - 2 books, DVD + Posters - blended teams in schools.
- **Find Meaning in the Work** - CD & Manual/Curriculum - presentation ready!